This is a bright and breezy account of the complex life of Mary Stuart – Queen of Scots – and modern readers, especially those who come fresh to the story, will like the speed and authority of this version. It is a 'little book' as the title claims, but Mickey Mayhew understands the background and complexity to the life of one of Britain's best-known royals, and wears his knowledge lightly.

Philippa Gregory, author of
The Other Boleyn Girl and *The Other Queen*

First published 2015

The History Press
The Mill, Brimscombe Port
Stroud, Gloucestershire, GL5 2QG
www.thehistorypress.co.uk

© Mickey Mayhew, 2015

The right of Mickey Mayhew to be identified as the Author of this work has been asserted in accordance with the Copyright, Designs and Patents Act 1988.

British Library Cataloguing in Publication Data.
A catalogue record for this book is available from the British Library.

ISBN 978 0 7509 6151 6

Typesetting and origination by The History Press
Printed and bound in Great Britain by TJ International Ltd, Padstow.

THE LITTLE
BOOK OF
MARY
QUEEN
OF
SCOTS

MICKEY MAYHE

The
History
Press

Contents

Acknowledgements

The author would like to lavish particular praise on the following:

Cate Ludlow and Ruth Boyes at The History Press, for giving me
   this opportunity
Steve Forster, for his help and hard work
Margaret Lumsdaine, Syd Whitehead and all at the Marie Stuart Society
Jerry Ozaniec
Sam Critchlow
Friends of Sheffield Manor Lodge
Friends of Sheffield Castle, especially 'Big' Ron Clayton
The numerous guides and staff of Historic Scotland,
   English Heritage, and Historic Royal Palaces
Harbourmaster Bob (you know who you are!)
Lesley Smith at Tutbury Castle
Castle Farm Guest House, Fotheringay
Peter and Barbara Wall
Neil Bond (for passing Mary my way)
Frogg Moody and Sue Parry
Nicola and Dennis Baskerville
Workington Library
And, of course, the parents

All images are taken from the author's collection unless otherwise
indicated. Those credited as BLFC belong to the British Library
Flickr Collection.

Foreword

There are few more luminous characters in the history of the British Isles than Mary Queen of Scots. Her extraordinary tale in equal measure of adventure and tragedy has fascinated generations since her lifetime. For many, she is saintly and misunderstood, virtually abandoned to nearly nineteen years of wrongful imprisonment by her jealous and calculating royal cousin, Queen Elizabeth I of England. For others, she is a foolish and weak woman who fell in love too easily (and more than once) with ambitious men who would bring her, and her title, into disgrace and therefore deserved to be imprisoned.

These polarised views, evident for centuries, prove why Marie Stuart still holds, in her life story, an irresistible charm, and give writers the chance to reveal new evidence about her life. What is undeniable is her beauty, courage and the fact that she had more than one line of legitimate royal blood in her veins, making her not only stunning to behold but also a real challenge to the English throne. Her life was extraordinary, her imprisonment and horrific death tragic, but she casts a bright light on the political and social workings of Europe in the sixteenth century.

Mickey Mayhew is a talented and sensitive historian who has spent many years studying Mary Queen of Scots and this book, far from little, is the fruit of those long days of research.

Lesley Smith
Curator, Tutbury Castle
2015

Introduction

My intention in writing this book has been – besides documenting the fabulous disaster of Mary's life in a beginner-friendly format – to drag her kicking and screaming into the twenty-first century; in this endeavour I hope soon to be bolstered by the advent of The CW Television Network's teen drama *Reign* to our screens. Sadly the word count for this book prevented me from jotting out an idea of what Mary's list of Facebook 'friends' list might have looked like; one can imagine the number of times she might have sent a 'friend request' to her cousin Elizabeth I over the years, only to have the action politely ignored. Because let's face it, Mary really ought to be even more famous than she already is; she was a woman who could turn breaking a fingernail into an international incident, and the sort of scandal that finished off Anne Boleyn would barely have occupied her past breakfast. In modern terms she would be considered a diva of the highest order, prone to tears when she didn't get her way and given to outright fainting if she found herself face-to-face with downright disagreement. And almost above all else she was utterly outrageous; any woman who can stand accused – whether she was involved or not – of blowing up her camp conspirator of a husband so that she could marry the most macho man on her council deserves to be hauled up to the very top tier of fabulous femme fatales of the last 500 years or so. And where Mary is concerned that's barely the beginning; mass slaughter (the 'Rough Wooings'), plots, decoys, assassination letters hidden in beer barrels, stalkers, daring escapes … to drag out that old careworn cliché, if her life was put forward as the possible plot for a blockbuster movie it would probably be thrown out for being 'too far-fetched'.

To many people in the past, Mary's tale is one of hardship, loss, and woe; to me – and hopefully to you, the reader – modern life and a certain sense of irony has enabled me to see the amusing side of her story; an incorrigibly plotting personality, a woman who, when caught red-handed encouraging all-out invasion, proceeded on more than one occasion to lie her way out of it with barefaced cheek, and then have a hissy fit when her privileges were revoked as a result. Mary's height – she puts the 'high' in 'high maintenance' – and her sultry Scottish accent (that's what an eyewitness called it) meant she was a man-magnet in the way her cautious cousin Elizabeth I never was, and to tell the truth too much of the tale of Mary's downfall is due to that special sort of feminine jealousy. Elizabeth may have been successful, and Mary a failure, but what a magnificent, dramatic failure her life was; that we could all fumble the ball so spectacularly. And the big reason both queens have such a hold still in the popular imagination is because of the great 'what ifs' of their lives; was Elizabeth *really* a virgin? Was her mother Anne Boleyn really guilty of incest? And Mary has more mysteries than both of them put together. Did she really help do Darnley in? Did Bothwell really ravish her at Dunbar Castle? Did Shrewsbury really love her? Was she really up to her elbows in the Babington Plot? We'll likely never know, like JFK and Jack the Ripper and a million other mysteries, and that's the reason we keep reading, and why she won't ever die, not really.

Mickey Mayhew
Cheam
2015

1

Stewart
Scotland

Mary Queen of Scots was a Stewart, daughter of James V of Scotland and descended from the great Stewart clan, but to all intents and purposes what mattered dynastically in the great drama of her life was that she was also a scion of the house of Tudor. She was directly descended from Henry VII, the founder of perhaps the most famous royal dynasty in British history. Henry VII's daughter Margaret was Mary's grandmother, who was sent to Scotland to marry James IV, Mary's grandfather, in an attempt to unite the warring nations of England and Scotland. On top of that, Mary lived and died within the Tudor period, which is basically from the moment Henry VII won the Battle of Bosworth on 22 August 1485 and ascended to the throne, right up until the day Elizabeth I died, on 24 March 1603. So although her surname may be Stewart*, saying that Mary Queen of Scots isn't essentially a Tudor is a bit like saying Thomas Cromwell wasn't Tudor because he never married his master, Henry VIII. That means that the world into which Mary was born was as much a Tudor world as it was a Stewart one, and, apart from her sojourn in France, she lived basically a

---

*Mary was actually born with the surname spelled 'Stewart', but being brought up in France meant that she used the French spelling and signed herself 'Marie Stuart' for most of her life. On top of that when she married her second husband Henry Stuart, Lord Darnley, she became a 'Stuart' proper.

Tudor life. This was especially true when she came to England, where she experienced the pinnacle of Tudor existence, an Elizabethan life. An Elizabethan life can be differentiated from a Tudor life because Elizabeth I, Henry VIII's second daughter, is thought to have had such an impact on the world around her that her tenure on the throne of England takes its name directly from her, whereas her father's time isn't really referred to as 'Henrician'; not a bad achievement for an unwanted girl who was bastardised at the age of 3.

At the time of Mary's birth in 1542, Scotland was not seen as a terribly important territory on the world stage, at least not in political terms, and not much more so on the great European stage either. Europe was mainly dominated by France and Spain, and to a lesser extent England. But Scotland was of great strategic importance where England was concerned because it was a back door by which other countries might invade. On top of this another problem, as far as the English were concerned, was the 'auld alliance' between France and Scotland, which can trace its official origins to 1295 and was renewed periodically thereafter; the common

A STEW OF STUARTS

The Stewart dynasty was founded by Robert II of Scotland, the grandson of Robert the Bruce, and the dynasty ruled Scotland until 1603, when, on the death of the Tudor queen Elizabeth I, James VI/I – Mary's son – united the warring countries of Scotland and England. The Stuart line continued, with Mary Queen of Scots' grandson Charles I falling foul of Oliver Cromwell and basically bringing about the English Civil War. The Stuarts survived, being brought back to a semblance of power with the Restoration. Eventually the Stuart line ended in 1707 when Queen Anne died without issue and the House of Hanover became the new ruling family. After the Tudors, the Stuarts are perhaps the most famous historical royal family in the country.

enemy in that regard was England itself. Although Scotland and England were natural enemies and had been for several centuries, England had always held great sway over Scotland by the simple virtue of being both bigger and richer, thus enabling the English to bribe some of the lords and nobles of Scotland and keep them in their pockets. Mary's third husband, Bothwell, was one of the few Scots nobles immune to such persuasions and on one occasion aroused the indignity of his fellow nobles by making away with some English cash sent to help overthrow the rule of Mary's mother, Mary of Guise; instead of helping to cripple her, the cash was a welcome present for her depleted coffers.

Mary's Scotland

The Scotland into which Mary was born was mainly rural, with a rugged, almost desolate and largely treeless landscape. There were many small villages, and these were in the main gathered around the many castles that peppered the landscape, thus creating small towns. Stewart Scotland was also still deeply feudal, not to mention being colder, wetter, and far windier than England, and on the whole it was a great deal poorer as well. The feudal aspect of Stewart Scotland was especially true in the north, where the power of the sovereign was delegated down to the great lords who ruled in those remote regions. In these areas the clan was the focal point around which society ordered itself, and often these were self-regulated systems, which resented interference from the main governmental body. In many respects they were run in the same way that modern-day gangs are now structured; the honour of the clan was paramount, and any attacks on that honour by rival clans/gangs could result in the most vicious and destructive of reprisals. Because of this the northern Scots were said to be a wild and barbarous bunch, who spoke their own tongue and whose sole allegiance was to their clan chief above all else. As far as their dress was concerned these men were bare below the knee and perhaps the only truly kilted citizens of Stewart Scotland during

Mary's day, despite what countless postcards and Hollywood movies portray. Down in the south it was a somewhat different story, with the border lands between Scotland and England an almost lawless terrain; some of the bad feeling between Scotland and England stemmed from raids committed by both sides in these border lands. The men who carried out these raids were called Reivers, outlaws with wild names and even wilder reputations, who lived hard, fast lives and usually died hard, fast deaths. As well as being a fierce patriot Mary's third husband Bothwell was also to all intents and purposes a Reiver.

In a troubled and violent era, the punishments meted out to offenders could be vicious. For poaching, people would have their ears nailed to nearby trees and then sliced off; for a second offence they would have one of their hands cut off. Banishment was an even worse punishment, because there would be no way for the offender to make a living once they had been ejected from the town, with neighbouring towns almost always unwilling to offer succour to those slung out from somewhere else. People caught committing adultery could be put in the stocks or subjected to some other form of public humiliation, sometimes having an iron collar put about their necks which could then be attached to a variety of places, from a church door to a simple pike in the ground, positioned so that they could neither stand, sit or even lean for a little respite. Punishments for wounding in a brawl or duel could be as severe as having the self-same wound inflicted on oneself by the person already wounded. For witchcraft the traditional punishments were either burning or drowning, Stewart Scotland having a particular terror for these sorts of supernatural mischief; Mary's son James VI/I was famous for his fear of witchcraft, going so far as to write the book *Daemonologie* in 1597, ten years after Mary was executed. *Daemonologie* encouraged the rooting out of witches.

Most people in rural Scotland still lived in huts with thatched roofs, the doors usually a simple flap of ox-hide; the entire family inhabited one room and usually shared the living space with any livestock they owned as well. The gap between rich and poor was, in fact, more akin to a yawning chasm; even owning something as simple as a stool was a sign of relative wealth, whereas the houses of the rich and the nobility were lined with tapestries and ostentatious ornamentation. Common folk made their money by exporting wool, hides, fish and other sorts of meat, plus anything else saleable that they could get from the extremely rugged Scottish landscape. If you were a beggar then the best you could hope for was a licence to beg in a particular town, which was sometimes granted; often you could be branded on the cheek for your troubles.

The main fortifications were still castles, whereas in England and in France the Renaissance fashion was for far more elegant, palatial homes that were less fortified and more aesthetically pleasing. The English did still retain castles but the nobles lived in these less and less as time went on, and they were used increasingly as state prisons, as was the case with Mary's final imprisonment at Fotheringay Castle. Mary's grandfather James IV and her father James V increasingly introduced these Renaissance ideas of architecture into Scotland, especially James V, who married two French brides, the second of whom was Mary's mother, Mary of Guise.

Despite their grandeur many of these castles and palaces were cold and draughty, in fact far from comfortable at all, and besides this, hygiene became an issue after a couple of months in residence; so many people living in such close proximity meant that the castle or palace in question would have to be vacated in order for it to be cleansed or 'sweetened'. This had the advantage of allowing the monarch to see more of their public, as they moved from place to place. Keeping these castles and palaces heated was another headache, which is why many of the main rooms were actually on the small side; Mary's supper room in Holyrood Palace, site of the famous murder of her secretary David Rizzio, is barely big enough to swing a cat in, let alone a sword. But smaller rooms were much easier to heat.

Mary of Guise. (BLFC, 000585250)

Dung, Stench and Disease

There were no decent roads in Stewart Scotland as such, and the few that did exist were poorly maintained by the nobles whose job it was to see to such things, and as a result they were often impassable in bad weather. Walking along what passed for a road in one of the towns was an often perilous experience; the classic picture of people emptying their toilet pans down on to the street and often onto the heads of unsuspecting passers-by was in fact very much the norm. Those depositing their refuse were supposed to shout out the warning 'Gardy loo!' and any passing travellers were supposed to respond with, 'Hold your hand!' Either way the streets in these towns were sodden with refuse, both animal and human, and the smell must have been overpowering, although most would have been used to it. Those who could afford it carried with them pomanders, little metal balls held by a chain which was attached to the waist, the ball containing some sweet herb or substance that could be sniffed occasionally to help ward off the evil stink. Some farm animals often wandered freely along the streets, with pigs being a particular problem, although local children apparently enjoyed riding around on their backs!

The perils of falling faeces illustrate the fact that life in Stewart Scotland, life in general even, was hard, harsh, brutal and fairly fleeting as well. The mortality rate was high, and many children didn't make it out of infancy alive; the mother herself often wasn't so fortunate either. Even Mary Queen of Scots, with her exalted royal status, was sufficiently wary of the perils of childbirth to draw up a will beforehand, and to curse her husband for putting her in such a situation whilst in the middle of what turned out to be a very painful and protracted labour. Despite these perils a lot of people managed to live to a fair age, even by today's standards, although they tended to come from the upper classes; Bess of Hardwick, the wife of Mary's main custodian whilst she was a captive in England, outlived all of the main Tudors and didn't die until 1608, at the ripe old age of 87 (or thereabouts). Many modern diseases didn't exist back in Stewart Scotland, but in contrast the people suffered from ailments that today's society has simply eradicated through the simple use of drugs and vaccines. Worst of these sixteenth-century scourges was the dreaded 'Sweating Sickness', which could strike a person dead within the space of a day or so, and which could wipe out whole communities in a couple of weeks. Medicine was fairly primitive, with doctors believing that the body was governed by four specific 'humours': yellow bile, black bile, blood, and phlegm. These four humours were said to work in tandem with what were considered the four basic elements: fire, air, water, and earth. These humours were said to govern how a person both felt and behaved, and could be sent awry by exposure to bad air, the cold, and countless other things. Bloodletting was seen as the treatment for just about everything, and was the remedy for just about nothing. By modern standards the whole medical system was shockingly primitive, but many natural herbs and medicines were used to ease pain and discomfort and to a large extent they did work; whilst there may not have been penicillin and painkillers as we know them, there were a great many other ways in which people could ease their discomfort, one of which was alcohol.

Smallpox was another disease greatly feared in Stewart Scotland, and even if you survived it you were often left with a face full of pitted scars as a result. Mary caught it when she was young but lived and even managed to preserve her famous alabaster complexion as well, passing on the tale – but not the actual ingredients of the remedy that had saved her face – to Elizabeth I when she too was struck down with the disease. Because they were so misunderstood many diseases struck mortal terror into the hearts of whole communities, and as a result often stringent measures were taken to ensure that they didn't spread any further than they already had. The tailor David Duly was hanged because he passed among the general populace even though his wife was dangerously ill; whilst being strung up the rope broke and he fell and survived, and so some small mercy was shown to him when he was simply banished for the rest of his life instead. Possibly even more dreaded than smallpox was leprosy, which was still rife in Stewart Scotland at the time when Mary reigned. Those with the disease were confined to a lazar house, and only allowed to venture out in order to buy supplies on certain days of the week. Before the Reformation turned the whole of Scottish society on its head, the monks of the various monasteries were those who tended to the sick, and many of their buildings had hospitals attached to them, some of which survived even when the monasteries themselves were dissolved.

'The monstrous regiment of women'

Childbirth wasn't the only peril that women had to endure, either. They were treated as second-class citizens, effectively the property firstly of their families and then their husband, and any property they themselves might have owned or enjoyed became their husband's on their marriage as well. Even those women fortunate enough to be higher up the social ladder were still regarded as inferior, mere bartering pieces to be married off to maximum financial effect. Mary herself suffered a great deal because of this inconsistency between the sexes. To sum up the mood of Stewart Scotland towards women, the famous Protestant preacher John Knox published a pamphlet in 1558 entitled, 'The first blast of the trumpet against the monstrous regiment of women'. This was an attack on Mary's mother Mary of Guise, and also Mary Tudor, Henry VIII's daughter by Catherine of Aragon – 'Bloody Mary' – who was then Queen of England. It suggested that the rule of a woman was unnatural and a thing against God, and that it could be considered lawful for her subjects to overthrow her. In a turnaround from what might be considered the mores of the modern world in which we now live, it was women who were seen as the more sexually voracious of the species, and who had to be married off as soon as possible to stop their uncontrollable lusts from laying them bare to charges of sin and fornication. This was again something for which Mary and her reputation in particular would suffer when she began to experience marital problems.

THESE WOMBS THEY KEEP ON WALKIN'

As well as being considered the more sexually voracious of the species, women in the sixteenth century were also prone to suffering from what was known as 'wandering womb' syndrome. This was a theory that originated in ancient Greece and basically believed that the womb would go wandering around the woman's body of its own free will, pressing itself against other organs and causing all sorts of ailments, although for what reason was never quite clarified. Even as late as the sixteenth century this was still generally believed to be the case, until the invention of microscopes revealed that the womb was in fact actually attached to something and not really of a mind to go meandering off for a caper around the kidneys whenever it felt like it.

Men in Stewart Scotland were macho in a way that most modern people would find perhaps rather ridiculous, but perhaps a little disconcerting as well. They carried swords and daggers as a matter of course, and most, if not all disputes were settled through violence; Mary's third husband Bothwell, as well as being a patriot and a bit of a Reiver, was also famous for challenging anyone who disagreed with him to trial by combat. It was a man's world in all the ways that truly mattered. This was perhaps the main reason why society had so much trouble adjusting to the idea of a queen regnant with all her attendant airs and graces lording it over them. All of the various clan systems were always headed by men, and women were forbidden from rising to become chief of the clan, even if the current chieftain had no sons to speak of; in this way it wasn't much different from the way royalty regulated itself, although of course then a daughter could succeed to the throne, albeit often, as Mary's reign exemplified, with considerable difficulties.

The people of Stewart Scotland enjoyed their alcohol; they had to, because it was almost all that they drank, from morning until night. Water was considered too polluted to drink, although the waters at Buxton in Derbyshire, which Mary used several times during her long imprisonment in England, were considered so beneficial that patients were encouraged to imbibe as much as eight pints a day. On a normal basis the main drink was ale, and also wine, although wine was pricey and therefore mainly the province of the upper classes. Diets consisted mainly of fish, both fresh and salted, and included haddock, herrings and especially salmon; also meat, as well as grain, coarse barley breads and oatcakes; fruit and nuts, and sweetmeats and delicacies for those who could afford them. Seaweed was often eaten by people who lived on the coasts. Diets became more substantial and more choice was available the further up the social ladder you were; soups with various herbs and flavourings, venison, ox tongues, geese, fowls and capons, and other choice meats. Groceries included fruit and eggs, but vegetables were only used as ingredients for soups and stews, and never eaten on their own. The famous Scottish dish haggis was also eaten, the word 'haggis' actually being a corruption of the French word 'hachis', which means chopped meat. Mary would be served as many as thirty courses per sitting; the various choices would be paraded in front of her and she would point to those she wished and simply let pass by those that she did not. For those surrounding the queen the number of courses you were served depended on your station. Those sweetmeats and delicacies which were served for what we would consider 'dessert' consisted of jellies, candied fruits, and marzipan confections of various shapes and sizes. Breakfast was eaten very early in the morning, and the main meal was usually served before midday, followed by supper at around six o'clock in the evening.

Meats came from hunting, which was as much for survival as it was for sport; animal rights as such didn't even exist in Stewart Scotland, as animals were thought not to have souls. Mary enjoyed hunting a great deal but there are no records of her taking pleasure in the suffering of animals, unlike Elizabeth I, who was a great fan of bear-baiting in particular. Vast numbers of animals could be slaughtered during one of these hunts, often being driven into enclosures where they could be more easily picked off; on a visit to Scotland several centuries later Queen Victoria was told of the practice and was said to have been shocked at the barbarity of it. In the main it was the rich who hunted animals for sport; for the poor it was simply a matter of survival, protecting their livestock from foxes and wolves, although pastimes such as cockfighting were a cheaper way for the more modest social classes to enjoy a bit of fun at some innocent creature's expense. Mary's main custodian in England during her long captivity, the Earl of Shrewsbury, had a cockpit near his main residence of Sheffield Castle. Mary also kept many smaller animals as pets, notably her famous Skye terrier who made an unexpected appearance at her execution in Fotheringay Castle in 1587.

For other forms of recreation people played various games, but access to these was of course based upon where you stood in the social hierarchy; a family living in a dwelling on the raw landscape of the borders would have little access to golf clubs, but Mary Queen of Scots was able to play at golf on the sands at St Andrews; golf had its modern origins in early Stewart Scotland. She also played tennis at Falkland Palace, on what is considered to be one of the oldest surviving tennis courts in the world. Mary also played Pall Mall, which was an early form of croquet, as well as 'riding at the ring', whereby riders had to try and hook a suspended ring with their spear as they galloped past. She also witnessed a football match in the grounds of Carlisle Castle on her arrival in England; the ball was probably some form of material bound together by leather. Football had been around for a while by the time this game was played in the summer of 1568, but it was, like many other fun pastimes, frowned upon by the Reformation. This was especially true if it was played on a Sunday. Football in Stewart Scotland was a far livelier affair than the game people are used to in the present day, the rules and the conduct being a little more like rugby; the ball could be picked up, although unlike the gentleman's game punching and kicking were also allowed and it wasn't unheard of for people to be killed during a game. The average family living in a dwelling on the raw landscape of the Scottish Borders would be far more likely to use a pig's bladder as a football, or some random piece of wood as a sledge for when it had been snowing.

The Cross-dressing Queen

Mary also loved hawking, using a trained bird to hunt game. Jousting was still the main way for men of class to 'perform' but there are few records of the men of Mary's court partaking in it. However, it was still in fashion in France, and was the cause of the death of the French king Henry II whilst Mary was growing up there, a tragic accident that was to catapult her into the position of queen of that country. Dancing was one of Mary's favourite pastimes, and something that could be enjoyed by all of the social strata, although most common folk would have been unaware of the complex choreography of some of the dances that Mary had learnt in France, and which she brought back with her to Scotland. Masquing was another fashionable court pastime, where people dressed up as various mythological or Biblical characters, either to put on a play of some sort or often as a form of disguise, like a masked ball. Masquing was another of Mary's favourite pieces of fun; on occasion she and her ladies even dressed up as common folk and ventured out into the streets of Edinburgh in disguise, something her father James V had often done, in order that he might find out what the normal folk were saying and thinking. Mary also dressed up as a man on one or two of these impromptu excursions, and at almost 6 feet in height she would, from a distance, probably have been most convincing. For the more bawdy members of society, indoor entertainments could be found at the taverns which peppered the backstreets of the various larger towns. Brothels were big business, and among the more famous frequenters of these establishments was Mary's second husband Lord Darnley, although whether he enjoyed the favours of both sexes is still a matter of some debate.

When the weather was bad in Scotland, as it often was, Mary would enjoy indoor pastimes such as chess, backgammon, and dice. She also played billiards, often gambling on the outcome of the game; on one notable occasion she and her second husband Darnley lost out to one of her ladies-in-waiting, Mary Beaton, who was partnered – in more ways than one – with the English ambassador Thomas Randolph.

At the time of Mary Stewart's birth Edinburgh was – and still is – the capital of Scotland and this was Mary's main base of operations, residing most of the time at Holyrood Palace.

St Andrews and Aberdeen were initially more important trading posts, but Edinburgh soon overtook them once the royal court firmly settled there. In Mary's time Holyrood Palace actually stood outside the city, which was walled, with Edinburgh Castle being the main fortification within the precincts of the city itself. There were various gates – or ports, as they were called – to the city, one of the most important being the Netherbow Port, which was located some distance down the Royal Mile; today visitors can see the line in the road where the Netherbow Port stood – it is just a few yards down from John Knox's House on the Royal Mile, and right outside The World's End pub, which sports plenty of Mary portraits on its walls. The Potterrow Port stood near the site of Kirk O'Field, where Mary's second husband Lord Darnley was murdered.

Holyrood Palace. (Marie Stuart Society and Joan MacDonald)

There was no 'New Town' in the Edinburgh of Mary's time, the 'New Town' which is nowadays perhaps most famous for the busy shopping thoroughfare Princes Street, and for the Scottish National Portrait Gallery. In Mary's Edinburgh there was only the 'Old Town' and that was where all the action occurred, of which there was plenty during Mary's time on the throne, including murder, explosions, kidnap, and adultery. The main street in the Old Town is now called the Royal Mile, part of which is also called the Canongate, and this was also the central thoroughfare of the city in Mary's time. The houses here were built four and five storeys high, and leaned forward so that at the tops they almost touched each other. Whilst the Canongate itself was fairly clean, the side streets were said to be a mess of sewage and vermin, and these were where some of the less salubrious residences were to be found. Most of the main traders were located on the long road between Edinburgh Castle and Holyrood Palace, which was punctuated with several 'Trons'. 'Trons' were weighing beams in Scotland and many towns were named after them. In the Canongate there was the Salt Tron and the Butter Tron, both of which were fairly self-explanatory. There is also the Tron Kirk, a landmark church on the Royal Mile, although this was built long after Mary was dead.

Churches and religion played a massive part in society; in fact they all but governed every waking moment. Whereas many countries are now multi-faith, Stewart Scotland was a Catholic country at the time of Mary's birth, although by the time she returned from France it had become Protestant – at least in the south – and would remain so, even though Mary herself continued to practise Catholicism. This process from being a Catholic country to becoming a Protestant one was called the Scottish Reformation. One might say that most of the problems Mary encountered were down to this particular dichotomy, along with the many pitfalls that came about from being a female monarch. So virulent was the feeling against Catholicism by the time Mary returned to Scotland that the general public saw even the saying of the Mass as something of an abomination, and there were several ugly scuffles when Mary attempted to hold Mass, both in Edinburgh and in Stirling.

'The monstrous and huge dragon and mass of the earth'

The Reformation itself had begun in Europe with Martin Luther, John Calvin, and various other early Protestants. The movement was seen as a response to what was perceived as widespread corruption in the Catholic Church, and the sentiments were quickly taken up by various disgruntled sections of society, especially among the poor, who were witness to how much wealth the churches actually had. In the Catholic faith there were countless saints and many complex rituals, but these were seen as signs of what were called 'popery' by the new Protestant faith, who preferred a more simplified, personal form of worship. The Pope was increasingly seen as the 'anti-Christ'; during her captivity in Protestant England Mary was often referred to in such terms, with one MP calling her 'the monstrous and huge dragon and mass of the earth'. The dragon was one of the derogatory symbols of the Pope, often depicted as some sort of beast or serpent, often seven-headed. The Reformation took hold in England when Henry VIII cut the country off from the Catholic Church in order to divorce his first wife Catherine of Aragon, so that he could marry his mistress Anne Boleyn. He then tried to turn Scotland towards the Reformation as well, but James V – Mary's father – was having none of it. The process of Scotland becoming a Protestant country was then a slow one, but because of this it was also a much steadier, more linear affair than the carnage that accompanied the to-ing and fro-ing back between Reform and Catholicism which occurred in England for the next twenty years or so.

When James V died shortly after Mary's birth, his wife Mary of Guise fought a long battle to become regent of Scotland, an aim she eventually achieved, long after her daughter had been sent to

France to keep her safe from the hands of the grasping English. Mary of Guise was a Catholic, albeit a far more tolerant one than Henry VIII's daughter 'Bloody Mary' in England, who was, at roughly the same time Mary of Guise became regent of Scotland, burning Reformers by the bucketload. Unfortunately that tolerance on the part of Mary of Guise allowed the Reformers in Scotland to gain a real foothold, and when in England 'Bloody Mary' was succeeded by her Protestant half-sister Elizabeth in 1558 it seemed that there was no stopping the progress of the Reformation. Mary of Guise did her best to negotiate with the Reformers, who were now styling themselves as the Lords of the Congregation, but the admittedly unusual burning of an 80-year-old Reformer and ex-priest at St Andrews only added further fuel to their fire. Whilst all of this was going on, the young Mary Queen of Scots was growing up in the relatively peaceful and idyllic French court; France's own wars of religion were still a fair few years away.

Despite these disputes the daily presence of religion was still a source of great comfort to many in Stewart Scotland, as well as being something which could cause great division and internal strife within communities. Many of the northern areas remained Catholic whilst those in the south turned more rapidly toward Reform. Religious tolerance was an unknown concept in Stewart Scotland and the transition from the Catholic to the Protestant faith was fraught with personal difficulties. Up until the advent of the Scottish Reformation, much of the religious life had centred on the monasteries and the abbeys peppered across the landscape. These were run by monks or canons of the various orders, such as Cistercians and Augustinians; when these monasteries were dissolved after the Reformation took hold they were handed over to the nobles to run. These men were called 'commendators'. The monks or canons had worked the lands that they owned, and although some of the orders were insular in nature, they often tended to the spiritual needs of their local communities and were sorely missed by the ordinary folk of Stewart Scotland.

The Reformation may have swept aside all of the abuses committed by the Catholic Church but it also set aside a lot of the simple, fun things that everyday people took for granted as well. Christmas in particular came under constant attack, with those who took part in festive fun coming in for criticism from the Reformers, who would have preferred it if the occasion could have been abolished altogether.

PARTY POOPERS

There weren't many games to be played in Scotland during the time Mary was a child there, and certainly not when she returned to find it had changed from a Catholic to a Protestant country; this was down to the fact that most forms of recreation were, in fact, frowned upon when Scotland became a Protestant country. This isn't to say that the former Catholic status was one big party, but the regime change saw a more sober, even sombre attitude to such things, and as a result people could be put in prison just for staging a play on certain feast days. Such was their fervour that a law was even passed in 1575 that forbade clothes of bright colours, which were seen to allude to a certain lightness of the mind, and insisted that people wear various shades of black, brown or grey. People were encouraged to display an air of gravity and piety, something that Mary's half-brother James Stewart (later the Earl of Moray) was especially well versed in; such a dismal demeanour especially endeared him to the Protestant English, although Elizabeth I wasn't too keen on religious extremes, and had a personal loathing for the famous – and ferocious – Protestant preacher, John Knox.

On her way to Holyrood Palace for the first time on her return to Scotland, Mary is said to have pardoned a band of revellers, some of whom had been sentenced to death for staging a play based on the 'Robin Hood' legend. John Knox was particularly put out by the many masques and balls that Mary staged at Holyrood Palace, but it didn't deter her in the slightest; the 'party princess' was there to stay.

There was widespread belief in the power of God to cause natural disasters if he was displeased with his people; John Knox, who pretty much claimed to have his own personal hotline to the Almighty, would ascribe almost any natural act that caused trouble to the displeasure of God; when Mary Queen of Scots landed in Leith after returning from France, the weather was dull and overcast and Knox ascribed it to God's displeasure that their Catholic queen had returned to rule over them.

Witchcraft was outlawed; Mary passed a law against the practice during her reign, and before her, her father James V burnt Janet Douglas as a witch. Mary's son James VI/I was particularly virulent in rooting out malpractices of this vein. Mary's third husband Bothwell was widely believed to be a witch – or a warlock, as is the correct term for the male – as was his nephew, Sir Francis Bothwell.

2

Scotland's
Bonny Bairn

Mary Queen of Scots was born at Linlithgow Palace, a few miles
west of Edinburgh, on 8 December 1542 (it may actually have
been the 7th, depending on how fast despatches were delivered;
also the 8th was the Feast of the Immaculate Conception of the
Virgin Mary, which might have seemed more appropriate and
thus a little fiddling of dates was deemed feasible). She was the
sole surviving legitimate heir of King James V of Scotland and
his second wife, the French Mary of Guise. Their marriage had
been cemented as part of what was known as the 'auld alliance'
whereby Scotland and France aided each other in times of
trouble, that trouble usually being something of a particularly
English persuasion. Their two sons had died in infancy and
so the crown fell to their newborn girl Mary; six days after
she was born James V died, exhausted by the Battle of Solway
Moss, where his forces had received a sound thrashing at the
hands of his uncle, King Henry VIII of England. The Battle of
Solway Moss was part of a wider ongoing warfare between
Scotland and England, and particularly between James V and
Henry VIII. In the main this was down to the fact of James
refusing to follow his uncle's religious policy, and also for
leaving Henry hanging around in York earlier in the year
waiting for a meeting that the Scots king wasn't all that keen
on; James V's ancestor James I had famously been held captive
in England for years and James V wasn't about to end up in the
same way. By an awful sort of symmetry the same thing would,

however, end up befalling his newborn baby daughter, some twenty-six years later.

In a society moulded by men, girls were seen as the booby prize of the birthing room, and James, wallowing in self-pity in the fallout of Solway Moss and holed up at Falkland Palace, was said to have turned his head to the wall on hearing the news and remarked, 'It came w'a lass and it will go w'a lass.' And then he promptly died. It makes for a nice anecdote, but most historians agree he was probably too ill to succinctly part with such a snappy sound bite. But you never know – it might be true.

Scotland being much smaller than England, it wasn't long before the Scots were forced to concede Mary's hand in marriage to Henry VIII's son, the then 6 year old and decidedly sickly Edward VI. The Treaty of Greenwich was duly signed and not long after Mary was crowned Queen of Scots, sobbing throughout the ceremony, which was held at the slightly more fortified venue of Stirling Castle. The Scots weren't terribly keen on the proposed marriage, especially when the notorious Tudor tyrant began laying down his many stipulations, one of which included having Mary sent to England when she was a little older to be brought up in the English court; likewise Mary of Guise was told that in the meantime her access to her daughter was to be strictly limited. The Scots soon broke off the treaty and so Henry sent his soldiers into Scotland and commenced what have come to be known as the 'Rough Wooings', burning, pillaging and basically conducting a campaign of terror in order to bend the stubborn Scots to his will. The young Mary was sent to the peace and tranquillity of Inchmahome Priory to escape the worst of the plunder, a little island on a lake north of Glasgow, along with her four childhood companions, the famous 'Four Maries': Mary Seton, Mary Beaton, Mary Fleming, and Mary Livingston, all children of various noblewomen and affluent families. The stay with the Augustinian canons on the secluded little beauty spot was a brief one, but like much to do with Mary, it has since taken on almost mythical status.

BEASTLY BROTHER-IN-LAW

Henry VIII didn't conduct any of his 'Rough Wooings' in person; he was far too fat and infirm to even consider such a task, and so it fell to his former brother-in-law, Edward Seymour – the Duke of Somerset – to set out for Scotland on several occasions and wreak as much havoc as he and his forces possibly could. Edward Seymour was the brother of Henry's third wife Jane Seymour, and therefore uncle to the young Edward VI. On these forays of fear and intimidation the English, with Somerset at their head, burned and pillaged crops and destroyed countless villages and also some of Scotland's most famous abbeys, including Melrose Abbey. The English forces occupied Haddington and during the route of his rampage Somerset was so close to Stirling Castle, where Mary had been taken after Linlithgow, that it was decided to send her to Inchmahome Priory for safekeeping. The actor Max Brown played Edward Seymour in Showtime's hit series, *The Tudors*.

Whilst Mary was shuttled forth between Stirling Castle and Inchmahome Priory, her mother Mary of Guise was negotiating a deal with the French king, Henry II, by which Mary would be moved to the safety of France and would one day marry his son, the Dauphin Francis. The Battle of Pinkie, not far from Edinburgh, only strengthened their resolve, as the Scots suffered another devastating defeat at the hands of the English. Mary, as well as her Four Maries and a large retinue, set sail from Dumbarton Castle on the west coast of Scotland soon after, bidding a tearful farewell to her mother in the process. The little queen loved the sea journey despite the majority of her Scots shipmates being seasick; Mary Fleming's mother Lady Fleming, acting as Mary's governess, demanded to be put ashore at the earliest available opportunity and was politely told that she could stay where she was or take her chances and drown.

On arriving in France at the port of Roscoff, Mary made a slow progress to the court, where she met her French relatives on her mother's side, the Guises, as well as King Henry II, his wife Catherine de Medici, and Henry's eternally beautiful but much

Chateâu de Chambord. (BLFC, 002899489)

older mistress Diane de Poiters. Henry and Catherine's marriage was an arranged one, because although she wasn't of noble stock as such, the Medicis were a powerful and influential Italian family, and she was related to the Pope. Henry's true love was always to be his mistress Diane, whom his father had introduced him to when he was very young. Henry and Diane's initials were carved on countless surfaces in the many French chateaux and he often wore her favourite colours of black and white. The lavish French court was a world away from the cold, stony castles of Scotland, moving between various elegant palaces and chateaux including Blois, Saint-Germain, Fontainebleau, Chambord, Anet, and Amboise, many of these located in the lush Loire Valley.

'The Italian woman'

Although actually an anointed queen, Mary was effectively the pampered princess of the French court. She hit it off well with her young husband-to-be, Francis the Dauphin, who was rather short of stature, sickly, and somewhat sullen and serious as a result. This state of affairs wasn't entirely his fault; his mother, Catherine de Medici, had spent years trying to conceive and ingested all sorts of potions and pills in an attempt to fulfil what was then seen as the primary duty for a queen consort. Poor Catherine, known by the public as 'the Italian woman', was always eclipsed by her husband's beautiful mistress, Diane. Catherine kept herself discreetly in the background, biding her time, and would eventually effectively rule as regent for her subsequent sons Charles and Henry.

Rumour had it that Mary's first meeting with her didn't entirely go according to plan; Catherine was observing the children in the nursery when the young Mary indignantly asked her if she was aware that she was in the presence of the Queen of Scotland;

DIAMOND GUISES

Mary's maternal family were the Guises, one of the most powerful and influential families in the French aristocracy of the time. Mary's mother, Mary of Guise, was the eldest of twelve children who were born to Claude, Duke of Guise and his wife Antoinette. On her mother's side she was descended from the French king Louis IX or St Louis. Whilst the young Mary grew up in France she was closely mentored by her mother's two brothers, Charles – the Cardinal of Lorraine – and his older brother Francis, the Duke of Guise. The Guises circled so close to the throne of the ruling Valois family that they were often accused of being unduly ambitious. Charles, the Cardinal of Lorraine, paid particular attention to grooming Mary for the station to which he felt she was destined; that of queen of France. He was said to have been an incredibly attractive man, so hell-bent on the pursuit of pleasure that he was constantly seeking new physical sensations despite his churchly station. It has sometimes been said that he and Mary shared some sort of illicit, incestuous relationship – certainly her third husband Bothwell referred to it when slandering her character, long before he and Mary were actually married, although there is no factual evidence for the accusations.

Catherine retorted drily by asking the girl if she knew that she was in the presence of the Queen of France. Apparently Mary had been labouring under the impression that Diane de Poitiers was the queen. It's a fabulous little faux pas, but perhaps a fictional one. The royal nursery grew rapidly during the years Mary was in residence; there was Elisabeth and Claude, as well as Charles, who developed something of a crush on the young Queen of Scots. He had an unstable personality and frequently took his tantrums out on servants, pets, or anything else that came to hand. Another brother, Edward-Alexander, would eventually become Henry III; then there was little Hercule and also Margaret, or Margot, who would become the inspiration for many books, plays, and even a film – *La Reine Margot* – although her fame would never eclipse that of the little Scottish queen who had just arrived in the country.

Francis II of France, Mary's first husband. (Author's collection)

LADY MARMALADE

Mary was an instant hit at the French court, and spent the rest of her
childhood and most of her teenage years being feted for her beauty,
her grace, her musical accomplishments, and also for the fact that as
far as poets like du Bellay and Ronsard were concerned she seemed
to have been plucked not from soggy, wet Scotland but from the
very heavens themselves. A group of poets called the Pleiade, among
them du Bellay and Ronsard, made Mary the centre of most of their
outpourings, and both du Bellay and Ronsard were chosen to be
tutors for the royal children. So far was Mary's star in the ascendant
during these dreamy childhood years that it was even passed down
through legend that marmalade was discovered because a chef, whilst
dreaming of her magnificent beauty and mixing up a recipe to aid
her in one of her ailments, got carried away stirring his oranges until
they turned into a frothy version of the fruit preserve. Subsequent
research has traced the word's origins back to the fifteenth century,
but it was a mark of how much of an influence Mary's beauty had
on those around her, and on how luminescent was her legacy.

Back in England the death of Henry VIII in 1547 hadn't done
anything to ease the onslaught of the jilted English; the ascension
of the young new king, Edward VI, had seen his uncle, the Duke of
Somerset, resume the 'Rough Wooings' with a vengeance. As well as
the dynastic angle there was a religious aspect to these conflicts, with
the English wanting to impose the Reformation on the Scots, who at
this point were still Catholics; it would be thirteen long years after
Henry VIII died that Scotland would finally become a Protestant
country, although it would be a far more peaceful transition than
the one that went on in England. Edward VI himself died in 1553
and his half-sister Mary Tudor – 'Bloody Mary' – the disillusioned
daughter of Catherine of Aragon, came to the throne. She made it
her mission in life to attempt to drag England back into Catholicism
kicking and screaming. To this end she burnt hundreds of Protestants
at the stake, further alienating her subjects by marrying a foreigner –

Phillip II of Spain – and not a home-grown suitor as was suggested to her. Her half-sister Elizabeth, Henry VIII's daughter by Anne Boleyn, Catherine of Aragon's successor, was the focus – if not the actual instigator – for several of the plots against her. As a result, as well as spending a few months in the Tower of London, Elizabeth was eventually put under house arrest for much of the remainder of Mary's short and unhappy reign.

Meanwhile, in the rather more settled environment of staunchly Catholic France, Mary grew up from girlhood into a striking, almost 6-foot-tall young woman, with deep-set almond eyes and curling reddish brown/auburn hair that may have lightened as she got older; a lock of that hair preserved at Holyrood Palace is almost flaxen in appearance. She was highly energetic but prone to bouts of nervous exhaustion which would only worsen as she got older, but such spirits made her the ideal companion for the dull and sullen young Dauphin Francis. Although her time in France was relatively idyllic – at least in comparison to what came later – there were several little dramas which doubtless both alarmed and amused her over the years. Her governess Lady Fleming, Mary Fleming's mother, became pregnant by the king on one of the rare occasions when Diane de Poiters wasn't around to slake his thirst. Catherine de Medici and Diane de Poiters co-existed fairly peacefully and the former certainly didn't want to swap the latter for some flighty Scots noblewoman with loose morals and even looser lips; it wasn't long before Lady Fleming was boasting of how buoyant being impregnated by the royal seed made her feel. Together Catherine and Diane put their heads together and had her ejected from the court and sent back to Scotland under a cloud of shame. Mary's new governess was the distinctly less loveable Lady Parois.

Mary's mother, Mary of Guise came to visit her for almost a year, during which time a plot to poison the young Queen of Scots was foiled and the perpetrator duly executed. Tragedy struck for Mary of Guise shortly before her return to Scotland when her only surviving son, and one of Mary's many half-brothers, died in her arms. She was never to see her daughter again, either. By the time she left, King Henry was glad to see the back of her, as her demands for money to secure her position of regent in Scotland were beginning to grate.

WHAT DID SHE LOOK LIKE?

Mary Queen of Scots was said to be one of the great royal beauties of her time. When praising the virtues of royalty and other various nobles, courtiers were often encouraged to espouse what would today be considered 'spin', but where Mary was concerned apparently all of the praise that poured forth was, well, kosher. She had flawless milky white skin, which was the fashion for the day, supposedly so translucent that you could see the veins in her throat through it. As well as deep-set almond or hazel eyes and wavy reddish brown/auburn hair, Mary also had a long, almost swan-like neck and, being almost 6-feet tall, her limbs were long and her fingers exquisite; perfect for playing on the lute or the virginals.

All of this is well and good, but many of the portraits of Mary don't always play up this great beauty to its best effect. The best portraits of Mary are those done when she was at the French court, by François Clouet; these exquisite line drawings really do put paid to the myth that she was anything less than stunning. No reliably verified portraits exist of Mary during her time in Scotland after returning from France, and of her time in captivity there is only a miniature by Nicholas Hilliard and from that the famous (and frequent – there are many variations) 'Sheffield Portrait'. This shows a slim, regal Mary not entirely dissimilar to the young girl of the Clouet drawings, albeit in different attire and with a slightly worn look and a more aquiline nose. A major exhibition to celebrate Mary's life in Edinburgh's National Museum of Scotland featured a CGI recreation of what Mary might have looked like based on the amalgamation of all the various portraits of the Queen of Scots, contemporary or otherwise.

Lady in White

Mary's health sometimes gave the French courtiers cause for concern, as, aside from suffering bouts of nervous exhaustion, she was also prone to odd fainting fits and sickness, said to have been due to overeating the rich and sumptuous foods served up to her on a daily basis. She also suffered from many of the usual childhood ailments including smallpox and measles, several bouts of which had already occurred whilst she was still a young child in Scotland. Young Francis's health didn't improve as he grew up either but such concerns were waved away by courtiers and especially by the ambitious Guises; the couple were betrothed and then married at Notre Dame in 1558, in a lavish ceremony during which Mary shocked spectators by wearing white – traditional enough in present times but back then actually the French colour of mourning. It is likely that Mary chose white more to set off her perfect alabaster skin than to signal the fact that she was signing some sort of sexual death warrant by throwing in her lot with a puny, sickly boy barely half her size. Among the countless jewels she sported on that day was 'the Great Harry', an eye-watering diamond of enormous dimensions given to her by the king. Coins were thrown to the watching crowds during the ceremony and several people were crushed in the race to catch them.

Before the wedding Mary had signed a series of documents dictated to her by her Guise uncles, the wily Cardinal of Lorraine and the heroic Duke of Guise, whereby she would effectively cede Scotland to the French in the event of her death. Historians are divided over whether Mary was too young to know what she was signing or whether her renaissance education had fully equipped her to fathom the ramifications of the documents. Scotland was essentially hers to do with as she wished; at this point her mother was ruling it on her behalf and she didn't envisage ever going back there; it was still viewed as a backward and barbarous country and on the few occasions when Mary dressed up in Highland gear it seemed more to elicit a few laughs from her French family than to try and enlighten them in the ways of alternative cultures. In fact, on the eve of her wedding Mary most certainly had no inclination whatsoever to return to what she and the French saw as little more than a satellite; the idea would have been almost laughable to someone living in a court that was seen as the

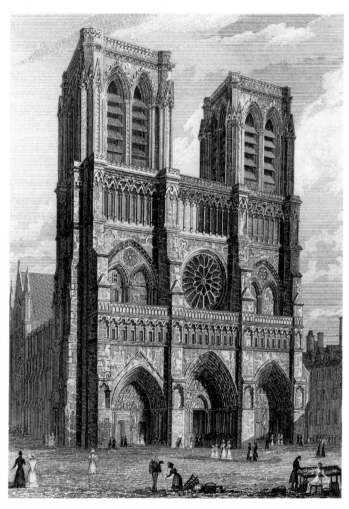

Notre Dame. (Library of Congress, LC-USZ62-115131)

highpoint of European culture. If anything, the French thought the Scots should be grateful to them for having saved their bacon from the savage onslaught of the English.

After the wedding there were several lavish banquets held in honour of the royal couple. Various of the younger princes rode to and fro before the court on hobby-horses, and then a series of galleons were pulled across a floor quickly carpeted with a large cloth, which was in turn pulled to and fro by more devoted lackeys so that it looked a little like the undulating waves of the sea. Henry II seated himself in one of these contraptions and invited the young Dauphiness Mary to join him, which must have been a great relief for the lackey who had spent the best part of the banquet holding aloft her crown above her head, as it had at that point become far too heavy for her to wear.

The young couple enjoyed their almost undoubtedly unconsummated honeymoon at the chateau of Villers-Cotterets, where they were shortly joined by the Cardinal of Lorraine, who was eager to see whether Francis would be able to sire the Guise/Valois child that would secure their position once and for all. In this he was to be crushingly disappointed, and it is reported that on several occasions he let the young Dauphin know just what a flop in the bedroom department he actually was. The king also visited the newlyweds whilst they were at Villers-Cotterets and decided that it would be best for Francis to 'man up' a little, and duly sent him off to the camp at Amiens. Mary was allowed the company of the Four Maries as a compensation.

In England, and several months after Mary and Francis's wedding, 'Bloody Mary' died and Henry VIII's second daughter Elizabeth I succeeded to the throne; almost at once began the battle between the two queens – Mary Queen of Scots and Elizabeth I – that would end in the former's death some twenty-nine years later, and which would become the subject of so many films, plays, and books. Elizabeth, whose mother was Anne Boleyn, was seen as illegitimate by most of Europe because Henry VIII had divorced the Catholic Catherine of Aragon to marry Anne; when the Pope had refused to accede to the divorce Henry had broken with Rome, setting in motion the English Reformation and the eventual creation of the Church of England, something that Elizabeth was brought up to believe in devoutly; she was in effect the child of the Reformation. But Mary and Elizabeth's respective childhoods were so utterly unalike as to furnish them for little else but a rivalry as they grew older; Mary had been feted and adored from the moment she

A QUESTION OF LEGITIMACY

To modern eyes and ears the endless Tudor disputes about legitimacy may seem somewhat trivial, but in an age when marriage and its offspring were seen as sacrosanct any taint of illegitimacy was taken extremely seriously, especially where royalty was concerned. As 1558 drew to a close the battle lines were drawn; on one side stood Mary Queen of Scots, a Catholic and therefore follower of a faith that stretched all the way back to Peter the Apostle – the first Pope – over 1,500 years earlier; and on the other side was Elizabeth I, a 'child of the Reformation' who had once been declared illegitimate.

However, Henry VIII had debarred his sister Margaret's Scottish descendants from ever inheriting the throne of England, preferring instead – in the event of the death of his own children – to pass the baton to the offspring of their younger sister Mary Tudor, who had first married the ageing Louis XII of France and then the Tudor hunk Sir Charles Brandon, best friend of the king. Mary Tudor's granddaughter was the famous Lady Jane Grey, the 'nine days queen' of England and in effect the first queen regnant since the somewhat questionable reign of Matilda in the twelfth century. Mary Queen of Scots endeavoured at various times to have this aspect of Henry VIII's will overturned. On her part Elizabeth was always famously touchy about the subject of her legitimacy, which may be one of the reasons why she so often cleaved to her father's memory whilst leaving her mother's, perhaps through political necessity, safely on the scaffold.

was born, but Elizabeth had been declared a bastard at the age of 3 when her mother was executed, and she spent most of the rest of her young adult life living on the periphery of the court, often coming into contact with her father or his many wives only when scandal came calling. Soon after her ascension to the throne of England, Elizabeth's legitimacy was called into question when in France Henry II maintained that Mary, as the legitimate – not to mention immaculate – Catholic descendant of Henry VII, was the true next-in-line to the English throne. He had her arms quartered with those of England as a way of putting his point across, something which caused deep offence to England's new and often insecure young queen. Once again historians are divided over how willingly Mary accepted this move, whether being the queen of two countries with the prospect of a third went to the head of a giddy young girl, or whether she may have perhaps had deep reservations about making such an antagonistic political move. She certainly maintained the latter stance in later years, when she was at the mercy of Elizabeth and her anti-Catholic courtiers.

Reign: The Teen Queen of France

Around eight months after Elizabeth I's accession to the throne of England, Henry II of France was killed in a jousting accident; a splinter of a lance entered both his eye and his throat, the wounds becoming infected, and as a result he died in great pain. Catherine de Medici claimed to have had a premonition about the accident but was unable to prevent her husband from breaking one final lance after what had already been an exhaustive round of jousting to celebrate, among other things, the outcome of the Treaty of Cateau-Cambrésis. This treaty saw an end to France's war with the Habsburgs of the Holy Roman Empire. Catherine believed deeply in the power of astrology and as well as having the Ruggieri brothers, Cosimo and Tommaso, brought to her from Italy, she also employed the services of that famous necromancer Nostradamus. But all her prophecies weren't enough to convince her husband that to continue jousting on that fateful day would lead to his untimely death. After ten days of pain and suffering in the Hôtel des Tournelles he died, and suddenly Mary, already Queen of Scotland, found herself catapulted onto the throne of France as queen at the tender age of sixteen. Her husband, the young, feeble Francis was now the king, crowned Francis II at Rheims shortly after, with his young wife watching. With the king dead Catherine de Medici extracted a dignified form of revenge on Henry's mistress Diane de Poiters, confiscating from her the chateau of Chenonceaux and giving her as recompense the rather drabber and reputedly unlucky Chaumont instead.

*Mary, Queen of Scots,
wife of François, Dauphin of France*

Mary's French Heraldry. (Marie Stuart Society)

NO TREATS IN THIS TREATY

The Treaty of Edinburgh was drawn up between the Elizabethan government, the representatives of Francis and Mary, and the new Scottish Reformation Parliament on 5 July 1560. It sought to abolish the 'auld alliance' between Scotland and France and set up a new one which was more favourable to England, and one that would be basically between themselves and the Scots. The Treaty of Edinburgh also sought to uphold the peace between England and France that had been agreed by the Treaty of Cateau-Cambrésis in 1559. As a result the French withdrew their garrisons from Scotland. Mary never ratified the treaty, perhaps because she viewed it as a validation of the rebels who had overthrown her mother's rule, and also because it declared Elizabeth the true and legitimate ruler of England, a subject that seemed to cause the Queen of Scots and the rest of Catholic Europe to raise an eyebrow whenever it was mentioned.

Mary didn't have long to enjoy life as the teen Queen of France; not long afterwards the Scottish Reformation Parliament ruled that Scotland was now a Protestant country, which meant that all her mother's efforts to hold it for her had essentially been in vain, exacerbated by Elizabeth I sending aid and arms to the reformers. The Treaty of Edinburgh was duly signed, whereby French troops withdrew from Scotland, and Mary and Francis were asked politely to stop quartering their arms with those of England. Mary of Guise had fought long and hard to maintain the status quo but in the end she was effectively trampled underfoot by the new wave of Protestantism espoused by the likes of John Knox, to the point where the Scots were willing to concede the help of their old enemies the English against her and her French soldiers.

Mary Queen of Scots had other problems to deal with as well as the ramifications of the Treaty of Edinburgh; an uprising in France whose purpose was to supplant the power of the Guises and replace them with a new Huguenot (Protestant) king – Francis was to be allowed to convert from Catholicism if he so wished – ended with a veritable massacre of the offending rebels in the courtyard at the chateau of Amboise. After dinner the ringleaders were first tortured and then hung from the battlements, so that the French court could enjoy their sufferings on a full stomach; many of the rebels were also thrown into the river to drown. Historians are divided on whether Mary was a witness to this spectacle, but given her sensitive nature when it came to scenes of carnage it may be safer to assume that she kept herself secreted in some back room with her eyes shut and her fingers stuck firmly in her ears. Another tale says that she witnessed some of the slaughter but begged to be excused, her husband making one defiant, manly stand as king and insisting to the Cardinal of Lorraine that they be given leave to withdraw.

Farewell Francis

Making matters worse, Mary of Guise died from dropsy whilst under siege from Protestant rebel lords in Edinburgh Castle; the news was kept from Mary for several weeks but she was absolutely prostrate with grief when she found out. Finally, in December of that year the frail Francis finally succumbed to an ear infection and died; cold weather whilst out hunting might have caused the problem, and the subsequent swelling grew behind his ear and then travelled to his brain despite having been lanced; it then became an abscess on the poor boy's brain. Like his father he was said to have suffered great agonies and torments before his eventual death. Mary sent for one of the best surgeons available, a French Protestant no less – or Huguenot, as they were referred to at the time – but Catherine de Medici intervened on the grounds that such an operation was out of the question. Whether she had finally decided to make a grasp for power by sacrificing one child so that she might be the brains behind the next one has been a matter of speculation, but whatever her motive the young Mary found herself moving rapidly from teen queen to teen widow in the space of a few short months.

As was the custom in the French court, Mary shut herself away for a period of forty days, during which time she mourned the loss perhaps not of a husband in the full, physical sense but more that of a cherished childhood companion and playmate. Despite this she was still a very marketable asset as far as the Guise family were concerned and various possible grooms were considered as they passed along the conveyor belt of European royal diplomacy in front of the grieving young widow. Eric XIV of Sweden and Frederick II of Denmark both made moves to make Mary their queen. At one point Mary very nearly ended up marrying Don Carlos, the son of Phillip II; her childhood friend Elisabeth of Valois was already Phillip's queen, and Catherine de Medici seems to have vetoed this idea on the grounds that it would eclipse the fortunes of her daughter. She may well have saved Mary from a fate almost as bad as the one that awaited her in Scotland, because Don Carlos had something approaching a hunchback and a tendency for torturing small animals; a fall down a flight of stairs whilst pursuing a serving wench only made matters worse and he was from that point onward a borderline psychotic. Although the negotiations faltered, Mary would attempt to revive them when she was back in Scotland. Don Carlos was the best possible catch in terms of prestige even if on a purely personal level he was about as desirable as death itself; in time he would turn his turgid passions in the direction of his mother-in-law, poor Elisabeth of Valois, as his madness grew.

At this time the English ambassador Nicholas Throckmorton attempted to press Mary to ratify the Treaty of Edinburgh, but Mary tactfully told him that she would need to consult with her family first. Throckmorton was impressed with the way Mary presented herself during her grieving, and saw that she was fast becoming an astute political mover in her own right. A famous painting exists of Mary at this time by François Clouet, showing her wearing the white mourning veil or *deuil blanc* for which the portrait is perhaps best known.

Whilst Mary could have enjoyed a comfortable, quiet existence living off her estates, or another prestigious marriage if she waited long enough, she instead made the decision – after the period of mourning had been observed – to return to Scotland at some point in the not too distant future. Her mother-in-law Catherine de Medici was apparently all too eager to send her on her way, and quickly quashed early rumours and also Guise ambitions that Mary might instead regain her throne by marrying Francis's younger brother Charles, the next-in-line. Mary's half-brother James Stewart, one of James V's many illegitimate offspring, came to France to brief her on her role

HE AIN'T HEAVY, HE'S MY BROTHER

James Stewart, later Earl of Moray and eventually also regent of Scotland, was Mary Queen of Scots' half-brother by their father James V, the product of a liaison between the king and Margaret Erskine, daughter of the 5th Lord Erskine. James was born with royal blood but the taint of bastardy meant that he was unable to ascend to the throne. Despite this the Scottish succession saw that even royal bastards were given beneficial treatment and the young James was appointed prior of St Andrews in Fife. He was a supporter of the Scottish Reformation and eventually became the leader of what were called 'The Lords of the Congregation'. He was quite prepared to tolerate his half-sister returning to rule, provided she kept her Catholicism to herself and allowed him to do all the real work. The Lords of the Congregation realised that having a comely young queen with a claim to the English throne was in fact an asset, even if she was a Catholic. Unfortunately for James it was inevitable that at some time after her return Mary would seek a husband, and one whose interests would perhaps clash with his own, either religiously or politically, or perhaps both. However, he was subtle enough to be able to ride out the mayhem caused by both of his half-sister's subsequent marriages.

and responsibilities on returning to Scotland, and to attempt to convert her to Protestantism in the process. In her turn Mary tried to convert him to Catholicism, even going so far as to promise him a cardinal's hat, but neither party was particularly successful in their ventures. Ever eager to please Elizabeth I, with whom he shared his Protestant leanings, James reported back on his meeting to Throckmorton, before stopping off in England on his way back to Scotland to stay with Elizabeth's chief advisor and secretary of state William Cecil. Despite this, Mary, at least in her early years, always cleaved to her half-brother in all things political, and perhaps foolishly imagined that he would nurture her in the same way that her mother's maternal family had. She would, in the long run, prove to be wrong on both counts, and where both her families were concerned.

After doing a sort of farewell tour of all her remaining Guise relatives Mary set sail for Scotland in August of 1561. She had requested a safe conduct from Elizabeth, who, being in a particularly catty mood, had refused to grant it unless Mary agreed to ratify the Treaty of Edinburgh. Mary gave her the political equivalent of the monarchical middle-finger and, bidding a tearful farewell to France, proceeded to sleep on the deck of the departing ship in order to keep the coastline of her beloved France in her sight for as long as possible; she also stipulated that the lash not be used on the oarsmen. Shortly before they set sail a large vessel had sunk in the harbour and all on board had been lost; those present had seen it as a bad omen. Mary took with her back to Scotland the Frenchified Four Maries, as well as a large retinue of her Guise relatives and various other courtiers, not to mention vast amounts of furniture, bedding, and even a stable of horses. There were rumours that Elizabeth might actually try to catch Mary as she made the crossing but in the end Elizabeth didn't get her hands on Mary at all; she did, however, manage to intercept the young queen's stable of horses during the crossing, although they were eventually returned to Mary at a later date.

3

Darnley, Bother and Bothwell

Mary Queen of Scots arrived back in Scotland on 19 August, sailing into Leith a little earlier than expected and under the cover of a deep sea mist that John Knox said was a bad omen for the country, a potent portent of doom on them for receiving a Catholic queen so soon after the Reformation. Her reception at Leith was decidedly muted to say the least, but she was given shelter at the humble nearby house of Andrew Lamb until her half-brother James and various other assorted nobles arrived to escort her to her main residence of Holyrood Palace. One story tells how Mary was so dispirited when she saw the selection of horses sent to convey her that she actually broke down and wept.

On her half-brother's sage advice the young Catholic queen had consented to leave the newly Protestant Scots to their own devices as far as religious matters were concerned, provided she herself was able to worship privately as a Catholic; Mary was marvellously forward-thinking in this respect, espousing religious tolerance in an age known for anything but. She even had a proclamation published making her views known, and this was read out to her dubious new subjects. Said new subjects responded by congregating under her windows at Holyrood Palace on her first night in Scotland and serenading her with a variety of sombre Scottish Protestant hymns, for which she graciously thanked them whilst perhaps wishing that they would thereafter toddle off and leave her in peace. Mary's wish to continue worshipping as a Catholic led to a few initial scuffles

Mary in Scotland. (Library of Congress, LC-DIG-pga-02493)

but her natural charm and youthful beauty soon won over the local populace. Her official entry into the city, processing down from Edinburgh Castle, was however fraught with pointedly Protestant iconography. Mary apparently put a brave face on it but can't have been best pleased to have a little boy, dressed as an angel, dangled before her eyes from out of a cloud whilst waving a Protestant Bible in her face. A re-enactment of a priest being put to the flames further down the procession was hastily replaced by one showing a trio of Israelites being burned for betraying Moses, a scenario which didn't seem to cause offence to either religion.

NOT FOR THE FAINT-HEARTED ...

Mary Queen of Scots is a mass of contradictions in most things, and when it comes to temperament and how she reacted in the face of fear and peril she is once more a riddle wrapped within an enigma. When people were rude or unkind to Mary, it was noted – especially on her return to Scotland, where Protestant iconography was rife – that she would sometimes swoon or even pass out in the face of such personal attacks on her religion. When fiery Protestant preacher John Knox harangued her, she famously burst into tears, but again it seemed more a reaction to the attack on her religion and monarchical status than on her good self personally; Mary was always very careful in making sure that her regal status was both maintained and respected at all times. But whilst Mary might faint in the face of religious rancour, she was also a woman who could come back from having a loaded pistol held to her pregnant belly, then able to organise an escape within forty-eight hours, riding on horseback for 26 miles to escape the scene of the crime, and stopping only to be sick; a woman who could ride into battle with a pistol this time at her side; and a woman who could disguise herself as a boy and abseil down the back of the sheer wall of Borthwick Castle whilst round the other side her rebellious nobles were calling for her head. Such blatant contradictions have helped keep her in the eye of the historian for over 400 years, and the fascination shows no signs of subsiding now.

It wasn't long after returning to Scotland before Mary had her first audience with the notorious John Knox, the Protestant preacher whose way with words was such that he was able to reduce the Scots queen to tears on more than one occasion. Knox had been a notorious enemy of her mother, rather tactlessly proclaiming her death from dropsy – an abnormal accumulation of fluid – as being the judgement of God; he had also passed a similar sentence on the fate of poor young Francis and his infected ear, declaring that said ear had become infected because he refused to hear with it the true word of God. On their first meeting Knox and Mary argued mainly over matters of religion, although they also touched upon the issue of subjects resisting their sovereign (Knox told her the citizens of Edinburgh would support him rather than her). Knox said of Mary, 'If there be not in her a proud mind, a crafty wit and an indurate Heart Against God and His Truth, my judgement faileth me.' Eighteen months after their first encounter they were to have a second run-in, this time with Knox pouring scorn on what he saw as the 'sinful' activity of Mary's predilection for dancing, especially into the early hours; all her life Mary Queen of Scots kept the sort of hours that would do most modern day clubbers proud, either dancing, partying or even when in captivity playing cards until everyone else in residence had long since retired to bed. Knox also singled out the Four Maries during one of his spite-laden sermons, accusing Mary Livingston of marrying hastily because she was pregnant when in fact her first child wasn't born until well over nine months after the marriage. John Knox was one of the few people on whom Mary's legendary charm was almost entirely lost; he saw her sweet words as the serpentine expression of your average plaything of the Pope. Another scandal concerning an 'illicit' pregnancy gave him more fuel for his righteous fires; one of Mary's chamberwomen gave birth to a child in one of Holyrood's outhouses. The child

John Knox chastising Mary. (Library of Congress, LC-USZ62-5791)

FOXY KNOXY

Although he was a preacher who poured scorn on ideas of fun and frivolity, there were a few things about John Knox and his personal life that would have left the nobles of Scotland scratching their admittedly less impressive beards in amused derision. As well as having rumours circulate of an improper relationship with his first wife's mother, to whom he had acted as spiritual advisor, another scurrilous slur concerned the fact that, during Mary's personal reign, he took as his second wife a girl of just 17 years. This marriage, so declared his detractors, was little more than blatant lechery. The girl in question was one Margaret Stewart, and she wasn't the first teenager to be wedded to Knox; his first wife had been just 16 at the time of their marriage. This new marriage outraged Mary Queen of Scots, especially because the girl was actually a distant relation of hers. John Knox was 50 at the time. Whether or not the marriage was a happy one is open to debate – there isn't much in the way of evidence either way – but they did have three daughters. Some people – specifically Nicol Burne, an ardent enemy of the Reformers – thought that Knox had resorted to witchcraft to win himself such a nubile and beguiling young bride, claiming that by means of sorcery he had turned his 'decrepit' old body into that of a 'noble and lusty man'.

was then murdered and buried but the body was discovered and the culprits hanged. Knox blamed such an incident on the loose lifestyles supposedly espoused by the queen and her ladies.

William Cecil is Watching You

Mary left the running of the government to her half-brother James and also to William Maitland of Lethington, her secretary of state; he later married one of her Four Maries, Mary Fleming. Maitland was essentially the Scottish equivalent of Elizabeth I's chief advisor and secretary of state William Cecil. History has signed off on Cecil as being Mary's most implacable nemesis, although it probably wasn't a purely personal campaign on his part; Cecil had lived through the reign of terror brought about by Elizabeth's half-sister Mary Tudor – 'Bloody Mary' – and he most likely viewed any other Catholic queen as being a possibility for proceeding down the same dreadful path yet again. How much he was behind various attempts to destabilise Mary's rule in Scotland is uncertain, but Mary began the relationship – albeit unwittingly, perhaps – on a bad footing by having her arms quartered with those of England whilst she was in France. Cecil – not to mention Elizabeth – never forgot it. Maitland and Cecil corresponded regularly with the consent of their respective queens, but Mary never enjoyed the close, trusting relationship with her chief advisor that Elizabeth I did with Cecil. The main fear from England seemed to be that Mary would attempt to impose Catholicism on Scotland, perhaps with French help; her immediate show of tolerance seems to have fallen flat as far as the English were concerned. As well as that there was always the matter of Mary ratifying the Treaty of Edinburgh ...

Mary went on progress around Scotland not long after returning from France – the first of many during the early years of her reign – the better to get to know both her land and her subjects, and also to deal with the occasional civil unrest in the process. During one of these progresses she was able to bestow upon her half-brother James the title of Earl of Moray, a cushy little number that involved the distribution of a lot of lands that he had long been rather keen on acquiring. This came at the cost of aggravating one of her powerful Catholic families, the Huntlys, and as a result Mary faced the first real crisis of her Scottish reign.

As well as the Huntly fraças Mary also had to suffer the attentions of the equivalent of a sixteenth-century stalker, the French poet Chastelard, who had returned with her from France and who secreted himself under her bed on several occasions and was executed for his endeavours. Mary had danced with Chastelard in various court masques and they had even enjoyed a friendly, platonic kiss; the Stewart equivalent of a peck on the cheek, and all part of the courtly game of love. On his second attempt at surprising Mary he was only thwarted by the screams of the queen alerting her half-brother to her plight; Mary is said to have demanded that Moray run Chastelard through on the spot with his sword. For his part Chastelard either did it out of love or because he was a Huguenot who wanted to besmirch her carefully cultivated Catholic reputation. As he was executed at St Andrews he reputedly called out that she was 'the most beautiful and cruel princess in the world'; Mary was probably inclined to agree with the former statement but might have frowned a little as far as the latter was concerned.

Mary's uncle, the heroic Duke of Guise, was assassinated at around this time and this caused Mary intense grief. She slid into something of a depression and remarked on how lonely and isolated she felt. It was therefore natural that the search for a second husband for her should have intensified at this time, especially as three of the Four Maries were beginning to show signs of becoming romantically

A RIGHT ROYAL COCK-UP

George Gordon, 4th Earl of Huntly, was called 'the cock of the north', a nickname that was basically one big brag. He was a cousin of Mary's and was responsible for the first major civil unrest of her reign when she granted the title of the Earl of Moray to her half-brother; up until that time the title and its revenues had been enjoyed by Gordon's son, John. John Gordon, a real looker by all accounts, rose up in revolt and even planned to kidnap the queen and force her to marry him; perhaps this was where Mary's third husband Bothwell first got the idea from. Mary declared both George Gordon and his son John outlaws and they were vanquished in the Battle of Corrichie; beforehand Mary had expressed her delight at being out in the field of battle and wished that she could sleep under the stars the way her soldiers did. George Gordon died from a seizure during the battle and tumbled from his horse. John Gordon was executed in Aberdeen.

involved, despite having apparently sworn a bond of chastity with their mistress, whereby they wouldn't get married until she did.

A Tale of Two Queens

Mary and Elizabeth I corresponded fairly cordially during the early years of their respective reigns, and several attempts were made at setting up a meeting, most of which fell through mainly because of discord in France; Elizabeth couldn't be seen hobnobbing with a Catholic queen when she was sending aid to French Huguenots. Mary, who wanted to secure her succession rights with Elizabeth (one may argue that she was in fact borderline obsessive over the fact), was understandably upset by the repeated cancellations. At one point they got as close as settling on York as a possible destination. They sent each other gifts as well as expressive letters often laced with some rather insincere signs of flattery. Mary waited ages for a portrait of Elizabeth to arrive. Despite Mary's best efforts – and also Maitland's, on her behalf – Elizabeth was clever enough not to want to name her successor, having seen how things had played out in her half-sister Mary's time, when she herself had been next-in-line to succeed and had been taken to the Tower of London for her suspected part in a plot to oust her. Also Elizabeth herself showed no inclination to marry, perhaps wanting to hold onto power without having a husband to answer to, whilst Mary began inspecting various suitors for her hand almost immediately on returning to Scotland. The Scottish ambassador James Melville cannily commented to Elizabeth that he knew that whilst she remained unmarried she was both king and queen of her realm, and that he knew she wanted to keep it that way.

For her part in the marriage negotiations Elizabeth wanted Mary to marry someone who wouldn't prove a threat to her country and its newly regained Protestant religion, even suggesting her very own master of the horse Robert Dudley as a husband. Dudley was tall, athletic and good-looking, but he was also the

VIRGIN ON THE RIDICULOUS

Elizabeth I's most famous sobriquet is of course 'the virgin queen',
and for centuries historians have argued over whether that description
is true. Many possible theories have evolved over the years, including
a wish to distance herself from her mother Anne Boleyn's salacious
memory; a wish to hold onto power alone and not share it with a
husband who would eclipse her; or even that she was in fact a man and
had been somehow smuggled into the cradle after the actual girl Anne
Boleyn bore had died when she was young. Court gossip, of which
Mary was to hear much during her English captivity, even said that
Elizabeth 'wasn't like other women' anatomically, which means that
another possible theory for her reluctance to take a husband may have
been the fact that she suffered from some condition or even a genital
deformity, although when she was displayed as a baby to ambassadors
no deformity was detected; it may possibly have been internal, but even
in later years her physicians were at great pains to confirm that she was
able to reproduce children. Again, we are taking the word of doctors
from over 400 years ago whose methods were not exactly foolproof.
However, her dalliances with her favourite Robert Dudley were at the
time more scandalous than anything Mary ever got up to; Mary even
remarked that Elizabeth had conspired with Dudley to kill Dudley's wife
so that they could get married, and she wasn't the only one who said so.
Over the years Elizabeth played the marriage game to great effect, using
the promise of her much vaunted virginity as a political bargaining tool.
During negotiations with Francis, Duke of Anjou she might have almost
reached the point of marrying, but was stopped by her ministers because
her prospective groom was a Catholic. Whatever the truth, history has
proved Elizabeth's reign to be a staggering success, or, as Mary herself
put it in the 1936 Katharine Hepburn movie, 'a magnificent failure'.

son of a convicted traitor and had at that time no titles of his own.
This was something a woman of Mary's rank took as rather an
insult, especially as rumour had it that Dudley was also Elizabeth's
cast-off lover; their indiscretions had been the talk of Europe for

years, not to mention the fact that his wife had died in very suspicious circumstances. Whatever else he was, Robert Dudley was certainly Elizabeth's lifelong favourite, but any potential union had been postponed when that aforementioned wife had been found dead at the bottom of a flight of stairs, with word quickly going around that he had had her assassinated so that he could marry the queen. Elizabeth had tactfully distanced herself from Dudley before her reputation was irreparably tarnished, a lesson Mary unfortunately either didn't or couldn't take to heart when she became embroiled in similar circumstances several years later. For his part Dudley himself apparently had no great desire to go to Scotland either; at this stage in his career as a professional wooer he had only been courting Elizabeth for three or four years, and her status as 'the virgin queen' was still some years ahead of her, despite a Commons speech to the contrary several years before. At one point, Elizabeth offered to recognise Mary as her heir as part of the Dudley marriage negotiations.

Enter Darnley

At around this time the young Henry Stuart, Lord Darnley, descended from the heavens and dashed aside all other possible suitors, essentially sweeping Mary off her feet in a whirlwind courtship that culminated in their marriage in July 1565; they'd first met – after a brief formal introduction in France several years earlier – at Wemyss Castle in Fife, in February of that year. Darnley was the son of Scotsman Matthew Stuart, Earl of Lennox, and Margaret Douglas, the niece of Henry VIII by his sister Margaret – Mary's grandmother – from her second marriage, to Archibald Douglas. Darnley's mother, Margaret Douglas, was therefore Mary's aunt; that made Mary and Darnley first cousins, but a quick dispensation from the Pope – which arrived after the wedding – soon cleared up this little inconvenience. Darnley was tall, good-looking and blond; not 'buff' in the traditional sense, but certainly well proportioned. Equally as important he possessed claims to both the Scottish and English thrones through his father and mother respectively.

Darnley, Mary's second husband. (BLFC, 000585250)

PUSHY PARENTS

Darnley's mother and father, Matthew Stuart and Margaret Douglas, had groomed their lad for a lofty office from an early age. Darnley actually first met Mary when she was in France, having been sent there to congratulate her on her accession to the throne. Matthew and Margaret schooled their eldest son to be a paragon of courtly virtue, but they also made sure that he was all too aware of his claim to the throne of England, and of the way in which he ought accordingly to be treated. It wasn't long after arriving in Scotland that his spoilt, sulky nature began to assert itself; it was said that his servants bore the marks of his frequent tantrums, and he was liable to throw a strop whenever he didn't get his own way. Even when he was married to Mary he continued to behave like a spoiled brat; whilst listening to John Knox preach, Darnley was flummoxed to hear the gist of the sermon being sent his way, with an accusation that 'women and boys' had been sent to rule over the good people of Edinburgh. Darnley promptly announced that he was going hawking and flounced out of the cathedral with as much noise as was possible.

Mary's ambassador to England, James Melville, considered him somewhat 'lady-faced' because at that time he didn't have a beard and the ability to grow one was seen as an essential perquisite for your average macho Stewart or Tudor male. One assumes that by the time he travelled to Scotland he had been able to sprout a bit of fluff at the very least, the better to impress Mary with.

Darnley's height was of especial allure to Mary, who, at almost 6 feet tall, towered over most of the men around her. Unfortunately for Mary, Darnley was also a childish, spiteful, dissolute drunk, and probably bisexual to boot; it has been said that he even shared his bed with Mary's secretary, David Rizzio. Whether Elizabeth I knew in fact what a drunken sot he was and sent him to Mary hoping he would be the ruin of her, or whether she was genuinely alarmed by the match and the implications it would have on her throne, with two descendants with Tudor blood in their veins, remains a contentious point over 400 years later. Mary's initial interest in Darnley may have morphed into downright passion after she nursed him through a bout of what was believed to be chickenpox whilst they were staying at Stirling Castle. In this case it is more than likely that chickenpox was actually an early stage sign of syphilis. Even now, with their courtship barely budding, Darnley began behaving like a real diva, boxing the ears of his servants and having a hissy fit whenever various Scottish

MARY QUEEN OF FROCKS!

To most people the classic image of Mary Queen of Scots is that of a woman in a long, sombre black gown, with a white ruff collar and a little cap trimmed with braid on her head, usually with a large crucifix hanging down almost to her waist; puffed sleeves trimmed with lace complete the picture. Nothing of her famous wavy auburn hair is visible save for the very edges below the little cap. Inventories of Mary's clothes show that she did possess a great many black garments, which she wore mainly for periods of mourning; these periods were closely observed and lasted traditionally for forty days. In an age of high mortality it helped that black was also extremely fashionable! Mary also possessed a large number of white garments, among them gowns, skirts and doublets, all of which set her skin tone off to greatest effect.

Mary's many dresses and robes were made of the richest materials available to her tailors: damask, satin, taffeta, silks, and velvets, with sleeves intricately embroidered, sometimes with pearls. Sleeves could be switched between various outfits and a sort of recycling system was often employed to allow for greater variety. On top of her vast collection of clothes Mary also possessed the royal jewels, the crowning glory of which was an enormous diamond called 'the Great Harry' and given to Mary by her future father-in-law Henry II before her wedding to the Dauphin in Notre Dame. She also had a string of extremely rare black pearls. Most of her jewels were stolen by her half-brother Moray after she was forced to abdicate, and given to his wife Agnes.

titles didn't come his way as quickly as he would have liked. He even
went so far as to slap the ageing Duke of Châtellerault on the head,
before making an enemy of Moray by suggesting that maybe he had
far more lands in Scotland than he was actually entitled to.

The 'Chaseabout Raid'

After Mary married Darnley, her half-brother Moray, now virtually
eclipsed from power, rebelled against them. Although Darnley wasn't
a Catholic as such, he certainly wasn't a Protestant either; in fact, his
allegiance seems to have been rather difficult to pin down successfully.
This, along with Darnley's tactless comments about the lands Moray
commanded, made Moray fear the marriage, not to mention the fact
that in England Elizabeth now seemed dead set against it. Moray was
'put to the horn' or outlawed by Mary and the royal couple set about
routing him in what became known as the 'Chaseabout Raid', with
the two opposing parties prancing back and forth between Edinburgh
and Glasgow without actually engaging in any combat whatsoever.
Mary wore a pistol for the occasion and Darnley sported a specially
sculpted breastplate in a half-hearted attempt to look more manly.
The rebels fled to England where Elizabeth secretly offered them
succour. She and Moray were old friends and he had for years kept
both her and Cecil constantly abreast of the goings-on in the Scottish
court. The outlawed Moray initially skulked around the borders and
at Newcastle after the Chaseabout Raid, waiting for the opportune
moment to return and inveigle himself somehow into the new regime.

Mary fell pregnant at some point during the Chaseabout Raid, but
by now her husband had shown his true colours and the marriage
was dissolving faster than one of her English cousin's apparently
unshakeable decisions. Darnley drank far too much, spent too
much time frequenting some of Edinburgh's less salubrious taverns,
and on one occasion was said to have done something so obscene
on a golf course that to this very day historians are undecided as
to exactly what it was, and who or what it involved. Such was

Darnley's disdain for doing any actual work that Mary was forced to whip up a stamp that could be used to sign documents because he couldn't be bothered to stick around long enough to do the job himself. In a similar vein a silver coin or 'ryal' that was minted for the happy couple was rapidly withdrawn from circulation because it showed his name in the ascendancy.

Among other problems also perturbing the royal pair, Darnley had become jealous of the sudden rise of Mary's Italian secretary, David Rizzio. Rizzio, initially hired because of his bass voice – Mary needed one to make up the numbers on her famous musical evenings – had come from humble beginnings as part of the train of the visiting Count de Moretto. As he was rumoured to be a hideous hunchback, it seems laughable that Mary would have dallied with the little Italian, which leads one to suspect that his Catholicism and proximity to the queen were more of a sticking point as far as the nobles were concerned. As the queen's cash began to flow into his coffers, Rizzio decked himself out in what he thought was a style fitting for one of such proximity to the royal person, and was by all accounts not above taking bribes from those who wanted an audience with her either. There was only one response for a man of Darnley's character, especially when egged on by various rebel lords with their own axes to grind: murder. In March 1566, David Rizzio was stabbed to death by a crowd of Scottish nobles. His portrait in Holyrood Palace, hung directly over the exact spot where his body was dumped after he was butchered, shows a far more fetching young man than contemporary reports describe, but it was painted long after his death and probably as part of the romantic cult that had sprung up concerning all things Mary.

Darnley soon lost his bottle after the awful murder of Rizzio; Mary must have sensed this because she played him like the virginals whilst she was held in Holyrood, wooing him with sweet words and even promising him a space in her bed for the night. She also convinced him that the rebel lords were planning to do away with him now that they were in control of the situation, and that they had no intention of delivering to him the crown matrimonial he had craved for so long. When Moray presented himself to her, Mary tearfully flung herself into his arms and remarked that had he been present in the palace she would not have been treated thus. However, it is

THE VOICE

Poor David Rizzio; little did he realise when he was plucked from the Count de Moretto's posse simply on the strength of his fine bass voice that he would end up as one of the more fantastic facts of the turbulent reign of his mistress. In one of the most famous murders in Scottish history, Rizzio fell victim to a mob led by the sinister warlock Lord Ruthven; the little Italian was dragged from the small supper room at Holyrood Palace where a select party was dining, among them Mary's half-sister Jean, the Countess of Argyll, and also Mary's master of the horse, Arthur Erskine, among others. In the eyes of the conspirators Rizzio had risen too far, and the fact that he was a foreigner and probably a Papist who spent far too much time playing cards with the queen didn't help matters much.

On the night in question, Saturday, 9 March 1566, Darnley arrived in the small supper room at Holyrood ahead of Lord Ruthven and the main mob, having let them in through the stairway that connected his chamber to Mary's. After Ruthven, in full armour and literally at death's door from a kidney complaint, had summoned the reluctant Rizzio from where he was cowering behind the queen, Mary was then restrained by Andrew Ker of Fawdonside, who held a pistol to her pregnant stomach as chaos broke loose in the very confined space of the supper room. The dining table was overturned in the confusion but the room – still visible today in Mary's apartments at Holyrood – remained lit by the fire which had been warming them on this cold Scottish winter's evening. The tapestries would have been set ablaze by the falling candles had not the Countess of Argyll snatched them up. Darnley himself shied away from taking part in the butchery that followed.

Rizzio's fingers were prised forth from their stranglehold on Mary's fabric and the little Italian was gouged out of the supper room; the first blow was apparently struck whilst he was still in there, as Mary said she felt the cold of the blade as it whistled over her shoulder. In the relative privacy of the presence chamber the real butchery began, with Darnley's knife stuck through Rizzio's corpse as a sort of signature, just in case there were any doubts as to who was behind the plot. Part of that plot may also have involved Mary miscarrying so that the rebel lords could rule with Darnley as their puppet king, but Mary put paid to that idea by being, despite her fantastically feminine façade, essentially as tough as old boots. Within the space of two days she'd won her hopeless husband over to her side and snuck out of Holyrood with him, having faked a miscarriage in order to get initial letters of help smuggled out to her few remaining loyal lords.

Today the body of David Rizzio is said to lie in the graveyard of the Canongate Kirk on the Royal Mile, but there are some doubts as to whether he would have been buried thus in a Protestant church; more likely, although not definite, is that he either remains in the unmarked grave by Holyrood Abbey into which he was first buried, or else, as some legends say, he was reinterred from there by Mary into the abbey itself to lie alongside her father, in which case his bones were probably taken away as souvenirs when it was ransacked.

more than likely that she strongly suspected his involvement – and it clearly wasn't just Darnley whom she had to fool.

With the help of Lady Huntly, whose initial suggestion of escape by lowering Mary some 20 feet out of a window whilst sat in a chair was rejected by the heavily pregnant queen, word was smuggled out of Holyrood about a plan for escape. After fleeing Holyrood, Mary – with Darnley and others of her entourage in tow – rode through the night some 25 miles, the queen stopping only occasionally to be sick.

Holyrood supper room (BLFC, 000185149)

After a quick stop at Seton Palace they reached Dunbar Castle, on the edge of the North Sea. This perilous escape was punctuated by the fact that Darnley, whipping Mary's horse on at regular intervals, yelled callously that if she miscarried they could always make another baby later on. On arrival at Dunbar, Mary proceeded to pause briefly between dramas to make everyone omelettes before writing to Elizabeth to inform her cousin of her current calamities; Elizabeth responded by saying that, had she been in Mary's position, she would have stuck her dagger in her despicable husband and been done with it. In actual fact the Rizzio plot had been known about in London beforehand, although whether Elizabeth herself was aware of it is the subject of some speculation; certainly Cecil seems to have been well informed, which was pretty much par for the course. A couple of days later the Rizzio rebels were routed, most of them fleeing into England, and Mary made her triumphant return to the capital, ensconcing herself in the more secure Edinburgh Castle to await the birth of her child and making her will in the process; childbirth was a risky business back then. Whilst the Rizzio rebels fled south, just to make sure that Mary got the message about who had been instrumental in her secretary's murder, they sent her the bond that Darnley had signed before the attack. Darnley, in the days that followed, became the very personification of *persona non grata*.

Mary's Boy Child

On 19 June 1566, after a difficult delivery during which a spell was cast on one of her ladies in a futile attempt to pass on to her the worst of the birth pains, Mary was delivered of a son, James. The baby was perfectly healthy and born with a caul over its face, which was said at the time to be a sign of good luck. On hearing of the baby's birth Elizabeth I reportedly sank to her knees in front of her astonished courtiers and proclaimed that 'the queen of Scots is delivered of a fair son, whilst I am but a barren stock', or words to that effect. Mary pointedly proclaimed Darnley's paternity of the child, just in case anyone suspected that he was in fact Rizzio's. Despite this, the marriage was all but irreparable by this point, and Mary became increasingly despondent as a result; she may have been suffering from postnatal depression on top of having a hopeless husband who'd been involved in the malicious murder of her secretary. She gathered together a new council, keeping her half-brother Moray close, most likely with a view to keeping an eye on him; their relationship had never really recovered after the events of the Chaseabout Raid.

Mary's son was christened at Stirling Castle in December, with Darnley refusing to attend the ceremony and generally throwing a monumental sulk, mainly because he was being blanked by the English ambassador; Elizabeth still wasn't happy about how the wedding had occurred, although she managed to put a lid on her temper enough to send a solid gold font as a christening present. In true Elizabeth style it turned up late but she covered herself by commenting wryly that Mary might make use of it for her next child. Elizabeth stood as godmother to the child, being represented in this respect by the Countess of Argyll as her proxy. Part of the christening ceremony involved the priest spitting in the baby's mouth, but Mary forbade this due to the fact that said priest was

WHATEVER HAPPENED TO THE FONT?!

Elizabeth I's christening present of a solid gold font was unusually extravagant for one of history's most famous misers, but what actually happened to the font after the christening? According to romantic fiction Bothwell – having become, after some very dramatic events, Mary's third husband – insisted it be melted down to buy troops, and this was why Mary was screaming and threatening to kill herself days after their wedding; one wonders whether or not she might have been happier had she married the font instead. Apparently it refused to melt; a bit like the woman who sent it.

supposed to be suffering from syphilis. The festivities cost so much that Mary was forced to levy a tax to pay for them, and the revelries almost scandalised the English when a masque featuring men with tails was seen as a blatant insult to the English; the slur was that all Englishmen supposedly had tails.

Bring on Bothwell!

A few months after her son's birth, whilst administering justice in Jedburgh, near the borders, Mary learnt of the serious wounding of one of her favourites – James Hepburn, the Earl of Bothwell. Bothwell, a brilliant bit of rough when compared to the flouncing Darnley, had been one of those who helped Mary recover Edinburgh after the murder of Rizzio; she gave him the wardship of Dunbar Castle as a reward for his efforts. Bothwell had also been fiercely loyal to her mother, but had a bit of a reputation as both a warrior and a womaniser. On hearing of Bothwell's brush with death, Mary rode out of Jedburgh to see him at his castle of Hermitage but on her return journey she fell from her horse into a mire and from there became so ill that she almost died. The spot where she fell is now known as 'The Queen's Mire' – and it was here that several of the items now on display in Mary Queen of Scots' House in Jedburgh were recovered.

THE BABY IN THE WALL

Rumours and relics circulate around Mary Queen of Scots, and so it's entirely natural that some of them should also circulate around her son. When she gave birth to James in Edinburgh Castle it was rumoured that he actually died in childbirth and another child, that of the Countess of Mar, was substituted to take his place. This seemed even more likely when the skeleton of a baby was found walled up in the castle in 1830 wrapped up in some old cloth. The bones weren't verified as belonging to a human but it seems unlikely that anyone would have buried an animal in such a way. Mary's chief biographer and passionate partisan Antonia Fraser put paid to the theory that it was actually Mary's baby, and the connecting conspiracy that James VI/I resembled the 2nd Earl of Mar because he was actually his brother; Lord Mar was made governor of the baby but this was a hereditary right and only to be expected. She stated that James also resembled his dad Darnley in some portraits and besides, with the interweaving of so many Scottish noble families, there might be a vague blood tie that would spring out in appearance a generation or two later anyway. Most exciting of all though is the fact that, like many of the rumours and relics coruscating around the queen of Scots, the real identity of the baby in the wall is impossible to prove, and therefore impossible to totally disprove as well …

For centuries historians have speculated on the nature of Mary's most persistent illness, which seems to have had its most serious flare-up at Jedburgh; throughout her life she often complained of a pain in her side and several diagnoses of porphyria have been administered retrospectively. Porphyria involves abdominal pain, vomiting, neuropathy and mental disturbances. Mary's great-great-great-great-great grandson George III was a famous sufferer ('The madness of King George'), and it has been speculated that Mary may have inherited the disease from her father, James V. She suffered what was possibly a second but less serious attack during the earlier years of her English captivity. That fall into almost certainly freezing water on the return from Hermitage

THE BOTHWELL BROMANCE

Bothwell's aggressive nature saw him make many enemies, and chief among them was Châtellerault, and particularly his son, the 3rd Earl of Arran. Early on in Mary's reign, Bothwell became embroiled in a sort of comic sexual escapade with Mary's half-brother John and her Guise uncle Rene, Marquis of Elboeuf, when they broke into the house of the Earl of Arran's mistress, Alison Craik. The fallout nearly filled the streets of Edinburgh with corpses, as men on both sides threatened violence. Bothwell and Arran eventually made amends, but unfortunately Arran then went insane: he became convinced that Bothwell was plotting to kidnap the queen. The mad earl was locked up but escaped, whilst Bothwell was sent to cool his heels in Edinburgh Castle. After escaping, Bothwell laid low for a while, although Moray sent a servant called Dandie Pringle to poison him. The attempt came to nothing. Bothwell fled Scotland but was caught by the English and did a stint in the Tower of London before eventually finding his way back to Edinburgh just in time for the Rizzio affair …

Bothwell, Mary's third husband. (Mary Evans
Picture Library 10578483)

might have led Mary to swallowing something which might have caused a serious infection, perhaps combining with pre-existing porphyria symptoms, and topped off with a nice heavy dose of Darnley-induced stress; perhaps seeing her beloved Bothwell on what might have been his deathbed didn't help either. On arriving back in Jedburgh she vomited copiously, almost went blind and then fell into a kind of coma where her limbs became so stiff that those around her feared that she had died. Her physician managed to save her life by binding her limbs tightly, pouring wine down her throat and then performing an enema. It might sound both harsh and primitive but it – or something, at least – worked, and the queen eventually made a full recovery.

In a side note, Moray, who had managed to evade implication in the Rizzio plot despite being involved in it up to his proverbial ruff collar, decided that this was the best time to go routing through her jewels in order to pick out the prize pieces.

From Jedburgh Mary eventually visited Craigmillar Castle, several miles away from Holyrood Palace on the other side of Arthur's Seat. She was still weak from the illness – whatever it was – that had almost killed her, and had fallen into an even deeper depression, lamenting the fact of her failed marriage and wishing that she were dead.

Darnley's Disaffection

A week or so after the christening, Mary pardoned the Rizzio plotters, the first pardon being issued on Christmas Eve. Mary did this – with some persuasion from her councillors – in an attempt to reconcile her lords, seeing the birth and christening of her son as the beginning of a fresh start for all of them. Such a pardon would also go down well with the English, and the Earl of Bedford worked alongside Mary to find a means by which the troublesome Treaty of Edinburgh could be set aside in favour of something a little more amenable to both parties. If Mary pardoned the Rizzio plotters, Bedford promised that Cecil would not hinder relations between the two queens. Of course, this didn't mean that the Rizzio plotters wouldn't cause trouble back in Scotland but they were prohibited from actually offending the queen's oculars by hanging around anywhere near the royal presence itself.

Darnley understandably took fright at this turn of events – he was number one on their hit list after having lost his bottle and betrayed them during the Rizzio affair – and so he retreated to his family stronghold in Glasgow. Shortly before this he threw a monumental hissy fit during a meeting where Mary had desperately tried to engender some sort of reconciliation; he flounced out in front of the queen and all her lords and told her in no uncertain terms that she wouldn't be seeing his face again for a long time. How right he was, although perhaps not in quite the way he'd expected; what was most likely syphilis took hold of the hapless Henry and that lovely face erupted with pustules and was probably permanently scarred as a result. Mercury was used to treat it and his gums swelled up and most of his teeth fell out, as a result of which he began to suffer from some seriously bad breath.

Despite being absent, Darnley was still causing trouble, writing to Rome and suggesting that Mary was not a good Catholic, and also cooking up several hare-brained schemes to invade England. Mary visited Darnley at Glasgow and somehow persuaded him to return with her to Edinburgh, perhaps out of genuine concern, or perhaps – aware that Darnley was forever shouting his mouth off about making a break for the Continent, or making veiled hints about his son's possibly suspect paternity – because it was safest to keep him close to her. The situation caused Mary's councillors, with Maitland at their head, to perhaps suggest that there might be some way of removing Darnley from the picture on a more permanent basis. Considering the fact that divorce was out of the question, given the resulting risk to the legitimacy of baby James, Mary must have realised there was no realistic way for Darnley to be removed other than to have him slain somehow. Though Mary was not present, Morton, Bothwell and Maitland met at Whittingehame Tower, and it is most likely here that the real details of an assassination plot began to take shape.

On arriving back in Edinburgh, Darnley was housed in the Old Provost's lodging at Kirk O'Field, a house within a pre-Reformation collegiate church quadrangle with the church itself, St Mary-in-the-Field, as its focal point. Kirk O'Field was on the site on which now stands the University of Edinburgh, a stone's throw from the Royal Mile itself and within easy walking distance of Holyrood. The Old Provost's lodging belonged to Robert Balfour, brother of Mary's former privy councillor Sir James Balfour. Darnley was at Kirk O'Field for a relatively short period of convalescence, with Mary making infrequent visits and staying the odd night, before the whole place was blown up by an enormous explosion in the early hours of 10 February 1567. His body, as well as that of his valet Taylor, were found in the adjacent gardens, but without a mark on them. The most likely explanation for this is that they were disturbed by the assassins whom eyewitnesses had seen swarming around the house; the two men made their escape through a window, from where they were promptly plucked and strangled as they descended into the gardens. A sketch of the crime scene was sent to Cecil in London and is now stored at the National Archives. Although Darnley and Taylor weren't in the house when it blew up, several of Darnley's servants were and they were killed by the explosion – although one lived to tell the tale. The entire house had been blown sky-high by the explosion, so that in Mary's own

Kirk O'Field sketch sent to Cecil. (Wellcome Library, London)

WHO DID DARNLEY IN?!

The death of Darnley is certainly Scotland's greatest murder mystery. Although the list of suspects is enormous, Bothwell's name was at the very top. It was later alleged that he brought gunpowder from Dunbar Castle and hid it in his apartments at Holyrood Palace; that he had been at Kirk O'Field that night, had lit the fuse – and had to be pulled back from inspecting it after it initially refused to flare.

Certainly James Balfour, a former secretary of Mary's, was involved. His brother owned some of the lodgings at Kirk O'Field, and he was supposedly the one who really procured the gunpowder, hiding it in the house next door to Darnley's. Darnley and his servant Taylor were then throttled by members of the Hamilton family, kinsmen of Darnley. Those living close to the murder site swore they heard the young king begging his 'kinsmen' for mercy ... A slipper belonging to another kinsman, Archibald Douglas, was allegedly found at the scene, although this discovery has been disputed by some quarters; would he have worn slippers with full body armour? Some suggest that the slippers may have been used to soften the tread of conspirators when surrounding the house. Archibald Douglas had cause to hate Darnley: he was one of the betrayed Rizzio conspirators.

Only one noble was ever to pay for his crime, albeit over a decade later – Morton. Many other confessions – mainly from Bothwell's men – were taken, almost all of them extracted under torture, but as they were obtained after Mary had left Scotland and her half-brother Moray was regent, no evidence about his possible involvement was ever revealed. Moray always kept clear of any commotion: he had made sure he wasn't in Edinburgh when Darnley was murdered.

words not one stone was left atop another. The list of suspects for Darnley's murder reads like a who's who of the Scottish nobility, but there was one name which stood head and shoulders above the others, in bright, bold capitals at the very top of that list: Bothwell.

Bothwell was sheriff of Edinburgh and it was his duty to take a squad of soldiers up to Kirk O'Field in order to see what had occurred. Darnley's body was removed from the scene of the crime and laid in the next-door new provost's lodging where it was examined by everyone from court officials to members of the general public. Several women who lived close by to Kirk O'Field were questioned about what they had heard but their depositions came a little too close to naming the true culprits and they were dismissed as having presented unreliable evidence. Darnley's body was removed to Holyrood and embalmed, and laid in state for several days; Mary was reported to have stared at it in a sort of dumbstruck trance which was probably plain and simple shock. Her mourning lasted little more than a few days before she attended a wedding and then took the air at nearby Seton Palace, the latter at least under orders from her doctors over concerns for her health. The wedding she attended was that of Margaret Carwood, one of Mary's bed-chamber women, and she may have felt obliged to show her face. Certainly the English court and indeed most of Europe were watching and waiting with bated breath to see what would happen next. Both Elizabeth I and Catherine de Medici wrote urging Mary to take swift action against the assassins, but by this time Mary's mental state was probably close to a nervous collapse, and she ignored their sage advice. Darnley was buried in Holyrood Abbey in the dead of night with practically no pomp whatsoever, some writers claiming that this was according to Protestant rites, and others that it was a sign of the general disregard he was held in.

The Mermaid and the Hare

Almost immediately placards began appearing around Edinburgh accusing Bothwell of the crime, some of them incriminating Mary as well. One in particular depicted her as a mermaid, which was at that time the common symbol of a prostitute. In this placard the mermaid was seen nestling above a hare in a circle of swords, the traditional Hepburn family crest; Bothwell was Mary's lover, the sign suggested, and she had murdered her hopeless husband in a crime of political and sexual passion. On top of this a strange, ghostly voice was said to be heard floating through the streets, accusing Bothwell of the crime and demanding that justice be done. On the insistence of Darnley's father Lennox, Bothwell was actually tried and acquitted of the crime. It didn't help that Bothwell had filled Edinburgh with his men, forcing Lennox to stay away from the city and thus miss the chance to present his case in person. Mary and Mary Fleming were seen waving to Bothwell from a window in Holyrood Palace as he prepared to make the short ride up the Canongate to answer his accusers, and an English envoy who attempted to see the queen to ask that the trial be postponed until Lennox could attend was left waiting for some considerable time, no doubt twiddling his fingers whilst taking in the impressive sight of nearby Arthur's Seat.

On 19 April Bothwell threw a Saturday night soirée with a difference, gathering together the various lords and nobles either at the elusive Ainslie's Tavern – historians can't quite agree on its exact location – or at his apartments in Holyrood Palace to sign a bond promising their backing when he proposed marriage to the queen. Anyone wanting a while to think about putting their signature to the bond was briefly reminded of the many intimidating soldiers Bothwell had positioned around either the tavern or his apartments, although a few nobles did manage to slip away, presumably when their host was a little the worse for drink. Among those who did put their names to the bond promising backing were Morton, Maitland, Huntly, Seton, and Lord Herries. Bothwell then put his suit of marriage and the bond to the queen whilst she was staying at Seton, but according to her later account of events Mary refused him, confused and uncertain over what course of action to take in order to quell the rising unrest in her realm. Maitland was with Bothwell on this visit to the queen at Seton and he was with her a few days later when Bothwell intercepted Mary with a large force on her way back from Stirling Castle where she had been visiting her baby son; she didn't know it but that visit was to be the last time she would ever see her child. Despite Mary being also accompanied by Huntly, James Melville and around thirty soldiers, no real resistance was offered. Bothwell informed the queen that there was a plot against her in Edinburgh and that he was taking her to Dunbar Castle for her own protection. Mary sent a man to the city to see if this was the case. By the time he discovered that it was not, the party were too far from the city walls for cannon fire to have any effect; the danger was that they might injure the queen whilst trying to come to her rescue.

Once at Dunbar Castle, Bothwell allegedly raped Mary. According to the law of the land, the only way for her to regain her honour would be to marry him. Mary later said of this time that whilst his actions were brutal his words to her were gentle. After a brief period of captivity at Dunbar Castle, Bothwell led Mary back into Edinburgh by the bridle of her horse, signifying his hold over her. He quickly procured a divorce from his wife; the marriage had been made for political and monetary reasons and there

RAPIST OR ROMANTIC HERO?

One thing historians can agree on is that James Hepburn, the Earl of Bothwell, Mary Queen of Scot's third husband, was a warrior. He was also a womaniser, someone who conducted extramarital affairs but someone who was fiercely loyal to Scotland, and especially to Mary's mother, Mary of Guise, during her own turbulent time as regent.

In the wake of the breakdown of Mary's disastrous marriage to Darnley, Bothwell is portrayed – mostly in fiction but also in a considerable amount of 'factual' evidence – as stepping into the breach, a real man who awoke real passion in the queen for the first time in her life. Antonia Fraser, in the introduction to the 2009 anniversary edition of her biography of Mary, admits to being influenced by Margaret Irwin's seduction scene in Irwin's novel *The Galliard*. The most damning evidence either for or against their relationship is what transpired at Dunbar Castle. James Melville was with Mary, and said Bothwell had lain with the queen against her will.

Others – faked Casket Letters included – said Mary colluded in the 'kidnap' and offered no resistance; that she had in fact known about it several days in advance. Perhaps she did: Fraser has suggested that Mary may have been willing to fake a kidnapping but wasn't prepared for the ravishment that followed. Other historians have argued that Mary made no attempt to escape from Dunbar when she was famous for her fast and savvy departures from dangerous situations, though Retha Warnicke maintains that given time she would have; it took Mary eleven months to escape Lochleven, after all. Either way, Mary would have been on her own: after the initial alarm had been sounded, no one came to her rescue. That Bothwell did indeed rape her is of course possible, perhaps even probable, though it does clash with his fierce loyalty to her mother. One also has to question James Melville's account too; was he telling the truth? He asserted that Mary had been ravished but was not among those who were made aware of the kidnap in advance, whereas Maitland was. Maitland did, however, shortly after defect so it may be possible that he considered kidnap one thing, but the actual ravishment quite another. Both cases are equally compelling, equally bogged down with discrepancies. In the absence of 'killer documents' turning up and telling historians the truth, you as a reader are simply encouraged to examine the evidence and make up your own mind.

was apparently little love lost on either side. Mary and Bothwell were wed shortly after their return to the capital. The Protestant wedding was a hurried affair, with little in the way of celebrations to accompany it. Soon Mary was calling for a dagger with which to kill herself, or failing that she was threatening to drown herself instead. She was traumatised perhaps for multiple reasons; for one thing her new husband was a Protestant and she had essentially betrayed her religion by marrying him in a Protestant ceremony; she may also have learned of the truth of his role in the murder of Darnley; plus of course the most obvious fact was that she may have been forced into the whole thing against her will. It was reported that Bothwell was insanely jealous of her, refusing her an audience with anyone where he himself was not present, and had guards posted outside the doors of her quarters. Coming from completely the other side of the story, it was alleged that Mary was insanely jealous of Bothwell in return, tormented by the fact that he kept his ex-wife in Crichton Castle and that he referred to the queen merely as his concubine. It is little wonder that over 400 years on historians are still attempting to untangle the knotted threads of this complex and contradictory couple. For those who believed her liaison with Bothwell was indeed the result of a passionate love affair, Mary's post-wedding traumas may also have come about because her marriage was apparently having the opposite effect to the unifying one she and Bothwell had both perhaps intended; by mid-June the nobility – Maitland among them – had turned against the presumptuous Bothwell and began to declare that they would rescue the helpless queen from his clutches.

Carberry Hill, Capture, and that Casket

As the situation in Edinburgh began to heat up, the newlyweds relocated to nearby Borthwick Castle. Here, after an initial skirmish – during which Mary escaped by disguising herself as a man and abseiling down the sheer side of the castle wall – the two sides confronted each other at Carberry Hill in Musselburgh just outside of Edinburgh, during the middle of a heatwave. Mary and Bothwell had been lured out of the relative safety of Dunbar Castle by Sir James Balfour, who had custodianship of Edinburgh Castle – granted to him by Bothwell – and who had promised to use its guns in their defence if only they would return to the capital. What the unhappy couple didn't know was that Balfour was now on the side of the rebel lords and was luring them into a trap, hoping that they would engage in battle with insufficient forces at their disposal. The rebel lords meanwhile had marched from Stirling Castle where they had been based, wielding a banner showing the infant Prince James mourning his father, with a little speech bubble in which the baby was seen to utter the words, 'Judge and revenge my cause, O lord'. Mary was wearing borrowed clothes because she had little in the way of possessions at Dunbar, coming to battle clad in a red petticoat with the sleeves tied with points, a partlet (ruff), a velvet hat and a muffler; her red skirt barely covered her knees.

As the sun beat down on both sides on Carberry Hill the willpower of Mary and Bothwell's men began to wilt, and they started to melt away. Bothwell strode back and forth from their vantage point, flexing his muscles and issuing forth various requests for personal combat which were passed along the chain of command among the cowardly rebel lords and then refused in a fashion that was almost comical, as well as being a deft delaying tactic. When a challenger was finally found he took so long limbering up for the combat that by the time he was ready to tussle the queen's forces had dwindled away to almost nothing; that was probably the point. The French ambassador du Croc was sent forward to parley with them and the queen was forced to secure her husband's safe passage as a condition of her surrender. It was one of those monumental misjudgements of character and situation that Mary was to make so often in her life: after an allegedly passionate embrace with his wife, Bothwell rode off in the direction of Dunbar; Mary was never to see him again. She was led down the hillside by veteran warrior Kirkcaldy of Grange, but far from the respectful welcome she thought she would be accorded, the soldiers of the opposing party instead hurled abuse at her as she was led towards the capital. A mob made up mainly of the citizens of Edinburgh met her as she was led into the town, pointedly passing the site of Kirk O'Field as they did so. The mob called her a whore and demanded that she be burned at the stake for the murder of her husband. Mary spent one dreadful night at the Black Turnpike on the Royal Mile, locked into a small room with no change of clothes and perhaps for the first time in her life no women to wait on her either. Several hours later she was so despairing of her situation that she is said to have almost flung herself out of the window overlooking the street, her hair askew and her breasts bared, begging the astonished crowd below for help. Following this ignominy she was taken briefly back to Holyrood Palace to be reunited with Mary Seton and Mary Livingston before being conducted to Lochleven Castle, a small, fortified structure on an island in the middle of a large lake in Kinross. Even on her way there, broken and betrayed, Mary didn't give up hope of rescue, deliberately slowing her horse down because she had heard rumours that a party of men were on their way to pluck her to freedom. Sadly it wasn't to be.

Not long after Mary was imprisoned on Lochleven a small silver casket was discovered by the rebel lords in Edinburgh, who had apprehended one of Bothwell's servants; the servant, George Dalgleish, led them to the location of the casket, which was forced open a day or so later and found to contain some letters, a series of sonnets, and several other important documents. This small silver casket and its contents were to have ramifications for Mary that would reverberate down through the centuries and are still the topic of debate today. At this particular point in her story they would, however, be tucked away until a better use could be found for them.

Once in Lochleven Mary was given over to the custodianship of Sir William Douglas, Moray's half-brother, and their mutual mother, Lady Margaret Erskine. The queen kept to her bed for almost a fortnight on arrival, refusing both food and water. She lay so still for so long that many of those on the island thought that she would die. It was little surprise that she miscarried Bothwell's twins several weeks later. Following on from that loss she was then forced to abdicate her crown under pain of being cut into pieces or perhaps cast into the lake to drown, or maybe even both; her rebellious lords were very inventive when it came to thinking up new and alarming ways of despatching people. Elizabeth I's ambassador Nicholas Throckmorton managed to smuggle a message to Mary concealed in the hilt of a sword, telling her that any such abdication secured through force would be rendered null and void, urging Mary to sign it simply to save her life. A few weeks later her son James was crowned king at Stirling with Moray modestly accepting the regency on his behalf; the cannons were fired in the castle grounds at Lochleven just to push the point home to the bewildered Mary.

THE LOST BABIES OF LOCHLEVEN

There has been much speculation as to the gestation of the twin boys
Mary miscarried at Lochleven, and how dating them might either
incriminate her in an adulterous liaison with Bothwell before he
kidnapped her and took her to Dunbar Castle, or else exonerate her if
the twins were found to have been conceived on or after that date, when
it is more likely that she may have been raped. If the foetuses were found
to date from the Dunbar episode, it still does not rule out a romantic
liaison but also equally validates the accusation of rape. Mary miscarried
some time shortly before 24 July; she was abducted by Bothwell and
taken to Dunbar Castle on 24 April, so if she did get pregnant at Dunbar
the foetuses were three months old; certainly they were recognisable
as being twins and as being boys. Although midwifery was old by the
time Mary miscarried, modern science might still have verified their
gestation period far more accurately than any eyewitness who may
have hurriedly cleared the poor things away. Aside from the fact that
they were twin boys there were no details as to how large they were.

A myth which sprang up in the aftermath of this miscarriage was
that the whole thing was in fact a red herring, and that Mary had
in fact given birth to a healthy baby girl who was smuggled off
the island and eventually ended up as a nun in France; the novel
Unknown to History deals with just this particular strand of 'faction'.
It was also suggested at a slightly later date that Mary bore George
'Pretty Geordie' Douglas a child but given the timescale and the
escape attempts this is rather unlikely. There is no contemporary
evidence for either of the surviving baby stories, but like all the
many myths about Mary, they are not entirely impossible either.

Moray visited Mary on Lochleven and gave her a stern talking to
about what a wayward queen she had been. The most faithful of the
Four Maries, Mary Seton, was sent to join her on the island, whilst
Sir William Douglas's younger brother George – 'Pretty Geordie' –
soon succumbed to her legendary charm; the cult of the tragic queen

was fast taking shape. It was even mooted that Mary might marry young George but Moray vetoed the idea, insisting that despite her blemished status such a union was still beneath his sister. Mary also managed to enchant young Willie Douglas, a tiny tearaway who was possibly the result of one of Sir William's illegitimate sexual exploits. Perhaps with Willie's connivance she made her first escape attempt disguised as a washerwoman, only to have her milky white hands harpoon the whole thing when the boatman spotted them sliding out from beneath her rather more convincing rags.

The Great Escape

A second attempt at escape from Lochleven on 2 May 1568, which involved drugging half the island with hearty doses of wine whilst young Willie Douglas pegged all the boats to the shore bar one, was markedly more successful. Once more in disguise, Mary walked out of the gates of the castle in full view, in the midst of the May Day festivities that the young boy had arranged, with himself cast as the 'Abbot of Unreason'. Dancing around the table in the great hall, he flung his handkerchief over the keys to the castle gates as Sir William Douglas dozed drunkenly beside them. Mary regained her freedom as a result of this highly daring escapade, having been on Lochleven for almost a year. George and Willie Douglas followed her to freedom and she was soon reunited with several of the noble lords who had held fast to her cause, and spirited away to the safety of the castle of Niddry. She enjoyed a little under a fortnight of her hard-won freedom before being beaten by her half-brother's forces in battle at the village of Langside, just outside of Glasgow. Watching from a nearby hill as her men were cut down in an ambush organised by Kirkcaldy of Grange, not to mention possible treachery and dissent within her own ranks, Mary for once lost her legendary bottle and broke into a cross-country flight that finally ended up in Dundrennan Abbey near the Solway Firth. From there, despite the protestations of the lord and nobles who had scarpered with her, she made the decision to cross into England and throw herself on her cousin

Elizabeth's mercy; this being the same Elizabeth who had expressed outrage at the way Mary had been manhandled by her nobles whilst at the same time engaging in a bidding war with Catherine de Medici to buy Mary's famous string of black pearls – Elizabeth won.

The small party comprising about fifteen or sixteen various Scottish lords and attendants, not to mention Mary herself, commandeered a small fishing boat from the commendator of the former Cistercian monastery, Edward Maxwell of Terregles. After much to-ing and fro-ing in regards to the fraught nature of her plan – the lords were far more of a mind that Mary should seek help from France – they set sail from the mouth of the Abbey Burnfoot, where the monks had once shipped out wool and other agricultural necessities to Europe. In order to get to England the party had to cross the Solway Firth, a journey that took them a little over four hours. During the crossing Mary apparently had a premonition of the awful fate that awaited her in England and demanded that the boat be turned so that they could make for France instead, but by that time powerful winds had taken hold of them and she was unable to escape her date with destiny.

Dundrennan Abbey. (BLFC, 001777997)

4

Temptress, Terrorist, or Tragic Queen?

On 16 May 1568, Mary Queen of Scots crossed the Solway Firth into England in a small fishing boat, landing somewhere just outside of Workington and gracefully tripping up as she disembarked; her attendants tactfully declared that such a mishap was in fact a sign that she had come to take possession of her realm. The locals – helped by a former French servant of Mary's – soon recognised the queen by her stature and porcelain beauty and word spread far and wide that the famous Scots queen with the racy reputation had landed on their doorsteps.

One of the men with Mary – Lord Herries – sent out a false story that he had brought a young lady to be betrothed to one of the sons of Henry Curwen, who owned the nearby property where Mary spent her first night on English soil. The Curwens were away but Herries was of sufficient status for the house to be put at his disposal. By 18 May, Mary had enjoyed her last two nights of freedom at Workington and then Cockermouth respectively and had been escorted from the latter to Carlisle Castle by Sir Richard Lowther, the deputy governor. From there Mary was given over to the custodianship of Sir Francis Knollys, who was aided in this task by Lord Henry Scrope. Although impressed by Mary's courage, charm and wit, Knollys was under instructions from a somewhat bemused and embarrassed English court to keep the Scots queen and her entourage under lock and key: she wasn't yet a prisoner but she wasn't quite a welcome guest in England either. Mary in England was a focal point for the

THE PREMIER LEAGUE

The strict captivity that would be the hallmark for most of the rest of Mary's life hadn't yet come into place during her weeks at Carlisle Castle, and among other outdoor recreations she was allowed to watch a football match played by twenty or so of her attendants on a green below the castle facing towards Scotland. This game is now apparently considered one of the earliest recorded football matches ever played on English soil, and Sir Francis Knollys was fair-minded enough to venture that there was no suggestion of foul play on the part of the participants, who were of course both spiritual and territorial interlopers into his sovereign's realm. Football was at the time a far rougher sport than the game played now, and the fact that players could pick up the ball, and punch and elbow their opponents out of the way, meant that it was played out rather more like a rough-house version of rugby.

disaffected Catholics who had never quite come to terms with the new Protestant regime. The fact that Mary was demanding help in returning to Scotland to overthrow Moray also put the English council into something of a quandary; if they didn't offer her the help she needed, there was always the chance she might try and seek it from France, and the English had no wish to see French feet back in Scotland.

Mary requested not only assistance but an audience with Elizabeth as well, and received a trunk full of secondhand garments for her troubles, a turn of events that so embarrassed Knollys that he maintained they had been meant for the lower ranks of her ladies instead. Mary was soon joined at Carlisle by more of her followers, including the faithful Mary Seton, who was able to rearrange her queen's dishevelled hair if nothing else, a talent for 'busking', as it was then known, that certainly impressed Knollys. Mary had cut her hair short during her flight south and it has been speculated that due to stress it never really grew back to any real extent, so she relied mostly then on hairpieces, not to mention the aforementioned Mary Seton's 'busking' skills. Most of Mary's followers were housed in the town although some of them were permitted to stay within the precincts of the castle. There were bars on Mary's windows and the outer rooms were packed with guards, whose footsteps kept her awake at night; this was to be a problem that would plague her throughout her captivity, for during her time with the Earl of Shrewsbury she would frequently be awoken by soldiers beating their drums outside her door at five o'clock in the morning. The fact that Mary still continued to keep late hours probably didn't help matters much.

HAIR TODAY, GONE TOMORROW

Mary's curling, faintly frizzy auburn locks were one of her most distinctive features, although they may have turned flaxen during later life. She cut her hair short on her flight into England and from that time on wore wigs of varying colours; stress seemed to have played a part in the fact that her hair never grew back properly again. These wigs were called 'perukes' or 'periwigs', and Mary had many of them, of various different colours and styles, as did Elizabeth I. They were so valuable that they were carried around in special bags. Whilst Mary Livingston was responsible for Queen Mary's jewellery, Mary Seton was responsible for styling her queen's hair and was said to be an expert 'busker', the term used at the time for what was essentially a professional hairstylist. A visitor to Mary when she was imprisoned at Tutbury Castle said she had black hair, but this was almost certainly a wig. When she was executed her head famously fell away from her wig and the executioner was left simply holding said wig in his hand. Today locks of Mary's hair are visible in both Holyrood Palace and Mary Queen of Scots' house in Jedburgh, both examples being of the flaxen variety.

Elizabeth, Cecil and Walsingham. (Wellcome Library, London)

On 13 July Mary was moved further from the border to Lord Scrope's Bolton Castle in Wensleydale, where she spent the next six months twiddling her thumbs and flirting with Protestantism whilst Elizabeth convened a hearing at York to determine her guilt or innocence in the matter of Darnley's death. Elizabeth declared to her 'dear sister' that only when that blemish was blotted out could she deem to receive her at court. Mary didn't want to move from Carlisle; it was close to the border and also part of a large town, so messengers could come and go fairly freely. Bolton Castle on the other hand was some 50 miles further into England and comparatively cut off. It wasn't near any major town and was accessible only to the somewhat hardier traveller. Mary apparently made one ill-fated attempted to escape from Bolton Castle during her stay, being lowered out of one of the windows by way of bedsheets to where a horse was waiting; the plan was discovered when one of her women – it was said to have been Mary Seton – fell off the stool she was standing on whilst waiting to be lowered down after her. Mary got about 2 miles away on horseback before Lord Scrope intercepted her, and the place where she was plucked from her abortive flight to freedom is now called 'The Queen's Gap'.

Fantastic Fourth?

Between October and December of that year the aforesaid commission was held in York to examine Mary's guilt regarding Darnley's death, during which Moray produced for the predilection of the English commissioners the infamous 'Casket Letters' as evidence. Stored in a silver box with an engraved 'F' for Francis on it, the 'Casket Letters' were a series of sonnets, love letters and marriage contracts said to have been written by Mary to Bothwell, mentioning both murder and Darnley's bad breath amongst other things. They were said to be evidence not only of Mary and Bothwell's adulterous passion but also of their plan to do

LOVE LETTERS, LARCENY, AND OUTRIGHT LIBEL

The Casket Letters are to Mary Queen of Scots what the accusations of adultery and incest were to Elizabeth I's mother Anne Boleyn; almost certainly an outrageous tissue of lies but impossible to quite conclusively prove as thus without access to contemporary evidence, and in both cases contemporary evidence is rather thin on the ground. They were discovered not long after Mary was incarcerated on Lochleven, intercepted when one of Bothwell's servants went to retrieve them. Bothwell's ownership of the letters has never really been in dispute, but whether Mary was the one who wrote them to him is another matter entirely. The original Casket Letters have long since vanished, and all that remain in the archives are copies in French and from French into Scots and also into English, and none of these is entirely accurate, not to mention the fact that many meanings are either warped or missed out entirely in translation. The veracity of the Casket Letters has been endlessly debated in the subsequent centuries since Mary's death.

After their first appearance at the York conference they were again displayed to the English commissioners when the conference was reconvened in Westminster. By this time Elizabeth had already assured Moray of the fact that Mary would not be restored to her Scottish throne. When Mary's commissioners were excluded from certain aspects of the proceedings, not to mention the fact that Mary herself was prohibited from attending, it was generally concluded that the trial was simply for show. It was said that Elizabeth herself was not personally convinced by the Casket Letters but that they were evidence enough to keep Mary where she was and to send Moray back to Scotland to continue as regent.

The Casket Letters were returned to Scotland and changed hands several times, residing eventually with the Earl of Gowrie, the son of the sinister Lord Ruthven who had led the attack on

David Rizzio. By the time Mary's son James came to power they had fallen into his hands and by 1584 he had most likely destroyed them. The supposed silver casket itself in which they were stored is now on display in Lennoxlove House in East Lothian, once the home of Maitland of Lethington. Today it is widely accepted – although not conclusively proved, as Elizabeth and her council would heartily concur – that the letters were forged, most likely originals sent from an unknown woman to Bothwell interpolated rather shoddily with letters from Mary who was writing herself either to Darnley or letters of a platonic nature to Bothwell. The most likely authors of these fabricated documents were either Maitland, Sir James Balfour, or even one of the queen's famous Four Maries, Mary Beaton.

away with Darnley, lousy breath and all. Although today they are widely believed to be forgeries, they were evidence enough for the English commissioners to decide to keep Mary a political prisoner in England, whilst Moray was sent back to Scotland to resume his regency, with £5,000 in his pocket as an incentive. It was during the York conference that a marriage was first mooted between Mary and the Duke of Norfolk, England's leading peer and also one of the commissioners for the English council. The fruits of this proposal would take several years to fully flourish, however; for now, and for Mary, the long, laborious years of her real captivity were about to begin. Perhaps sensing what lay ahead, Mary had to be all but prised from the battlements of Bolton Castle by her fingertips and escorted south to Tutbury Castle in Staffordshire, to be given over into the custodianship of the Earl and Countess of Shrewsbury.

George Talbot, 6th Earl of Shrewsbury and his wife, the hardnosed businesswoman better known to history as Bess of Hardwick, owned most of Derbyshire and were ideally situated both geographically and financially to preside over Mary's little 'mock court'. Since her flight into England this entourage had grown in size so that at this point it numbered around some sixty people or so, some of whom were considered merely hangers-on. The properties of the earl and his wife were far enough away from the coast to prevent any rescue attempts being made and also far enough away from the court in London for Elizabeth not to have to worry about running into her younger, more comely cousin.

Mary's entourage consisted of cooks and pages, ladies-in-waiting, an apothecary, and several grooms. Many of these people had their own servants and in some cases even had their own entire families in tow. All of them needed to be housed and fed and the Shrewsburys were probably the only ones in the country capable of affording it. Whatever else she thought of Mary, Elizabeth was adamant that she was to be treated in the manner of an anointed queen. This meant that as well as having attendants for almost every function she also sat under a cloth of state, and was served a staggering thirty-two courses for her dinner; people still bowed before her and she was basically allowed all the trappings of queenship, with the emphasis unfortunately on being 'trapped'.

From Tutbury to Wingfield

Tutbury Castle, to which Mary was first taken as a 'guest' of the Shrewsburys, was perhaps the worst of her prisons, used more as a hunting lodge by its owners than as an actual residence. In fact it was in dire need of a little TLC; the plasterwork was peeling and the draughts were diabolical. It wasn't long before Shrewsbury petitioned Elizabeth for a move to the more congenial surroundings of Wingfield Manor, an impressive fortified house several miles away, where Mary enjoyed greater freedom. Shrewsbury was taken ill during this initial outing to Wingfield and he and his wife received a sharp rebuke from Elizabeth for neglecting their duties as custodians by removing themselves from Mary's care in order to visit the curative waters at nearby Buxton.

Before long Mary was back at Tutbury and from thence she was taken to St Mary's Guildhall and various other residences in Coventry, after the outbreak of the Northern Rebellion or 'Rising of the North'. This rebellion, coming from the mainly Catholic north of the country, caused the council in London to fear that the rebels were marching south to free Mary and place her on the throne, doing away with the usurping Elizabeth in the process. Led by the disgruntled Catholic Earls of Northumberland and Westmorland, the rebellion petered out and the resulting reprisals were vicious to say the least; the lower classes were hanged in their hundreds, whilst the upper classes got away with just the odd forfeiture of land. By January 1570 Mary was back at Tutbury, at roughly the same time as her half-brother Moray was assassinated in her birth town of Linlithgow; Mary made sure the assassin got a good pension. Darnley's father Lennox became the new regent in his wake.

The Pope, Pius V, excommunicated Elizabeth I in the spring of 1570, giving all disgruntled English Catholics a reason for assassinating her and also absolution if they actually managed to do the deed; this turn of events actually proceeded to put Mary's life in greater peril as she became a focal point for plots against the government on which she was dependent for her life and well-being. Later Mary was moved to Chatsworth, the house Bess of Hardwick had helped build from the fruits of one of her many past marriages. Sir William Cecil visited Mary here with a proposition for her restitution but matters stalled as Elizabeth prevaricated, as was her nature. Here Mary embroidered a small tapestry depicting a malicious ginger cat with a poor, petrified mouse beneath its paw; this may also have referred to Bess, who shared Elizabeth's colouring. On 28 November Mary was transferred from Chatsworth to Shrewsbury's main home of Sheffield Castle, which, apart from the occasional sojourn whilst the castle was 'sweetened', was to be her main residence/prison for the next fourteen years or so. It was here that she became embroiled in the Ridolfi Plot, named after the Florentine banker Roberto Ridolfi; his was a plan – given full Papal backing – to depose Elizabeth and marry Mary to the premier peer of England, the Duke of Norfolk, whilst at the same time ensuring that the country was overwhelmed by an invading Catholic force. This marriage between Mary and the Duke of Norfolk had, as said, first been mooted whilst Mary had been held at Bolton Castle.

One of Ridolfi's men, Charles Baillie, was arrested at Dover and the secret ciphers he was carrying with him were seized; he was

THE ONE THAT GOT AWAY

Thomas Howard, 4th Duke of Norfolk, almost became the fourth husband of Mary Queen of Scots. He was the son of the famous poet and Tudor courtier Henry Howard, who had his head chopped off for attempting to kidnap the boy king Edward VI and use him to overthrow his father, Henry VIII. Despite this less than appealing pedigree Thomas Howard was the premier nobleman in Elizabeth I's court; he was also the queen's second cousin. Norfolk was a Protestant but had Catholic sympathies. He'd been widowed three times already before his sister, Lady Scrope, along with Maitland, suggested that he might marry Mary Queen of Scots and so become her fourth husband.

Norfolk was one of the commissioners at Mary's trial in York and whilst he professed to be horrified by the contents of the Casket Letters he still considered Maitland's proposal. Mary and Norfolk began corresponding, although they almost certainly never met. When Elizabeth got wind of the plan she promptly put Norfolk into the Tower of London; when he was released he immediately took up where he'd left off, this time becoming embroiled in the Ridolfi Plot. Both Norfolk and Ridolfi had had a hand in the Northern Rebellion. Pope Pius V was aware of the Ridolfi Plot, as was Phillip II, whose general, the Duke of Alva (or 'Alba'), was to invade England and overwhelm the country with a Catholic invasion.

made to decipher them after a few rapid sessions on the rack. Under threat of similar torture John Leslie, Bishop of Ross and also Mary's ambassador, blabbed the entire plot to the torturers whilst he was being held in the Tower of London. Norfolk was thrown back into the Tower and this time he was put on trial for treason and found guilty, although Elizabeth was to postpone his execution on several occasions. Mary's household was cut as a result of the ramifications of the Ridolfi Plot, and among those ordered from her service was her young hero from Lochleven, little Willie Douglas. Either out of pure spite or perhaps merely unstinting devotion to his mistress, Cecil had published various portions of the Casket Letters later in the year, making sure that Mary's was a name now synonymous with infamy and intrigue. There were calls for her to be executed but it was to Elizabeth's credit that she protected her cousin from the general outcry. On 2 June 1572 the Duke of Norfolk was, however, beheaded for his part in the Ridolfi Plot, the first nobleman to grace the scaffold in Elizabeth's relatively peaceful reign.

In August of the same year the Massacre of St Bartholomew's Eve occurred in France, with countless Huguenots slain by French Catholics, the atrocity further hardening English hearts against the captive Queen of Scots; a glaring example of guilt by association. The Earl of Morton succeeded Darnley's father Lennox as regent in Scotland, despite being part and parcel of the plot to kill both Rizzio and Darnley. Morton was no friend to Mary and this, as well as the fall of Edinburgh Castle, effectively saw an end to the small but determined party that had been holding out for her in Scotland for the past few years. Maitland was at their head – he had since switched sides again in the wake of Bothwell's departure and probably also persuaded by his wife, Mary Fleming – moving his loyalties once more firmly in line with Mary and, along with stalwart soldier Kirkcaldy of Grange, had been holed up in Edinburgh Castle. The opposing king's party petitioned Elizabeth for help and the English queen, in no mood to support her treacherous cousin, sent it to them. When Edinburgh Castle was besieged by the English, Kirkcaldy of Grange was captured and executed; Maitland either died of natural causes – he was wasting away with some sort of muscle deterioration at the time – or else he committed suicide. Mary took his death almost as badly as she had that of Norfolk; she had now lost two men crucial to her cause in a relatively short space of time, and various other Scottish nobles who had until recently been relatively loyal were now deserting her, as her situation seemed increasingly hopeless. The appointment of Morton as the new, ruthless regent seemed to cement her continual downward slide, not to mention the fact that her son was being brought up in the Protestant faith and being firmly indoctrinated with the idea that his absent mother was both a murderess and an adulteress.

George Talbot, 6th Earl of Shrewsbury. (J.D. Leader)

KEEPING UP WITH THE SHREWSBURYS

George Talbot, 6th Earl of Shrewsbury and his wife Bess of Hardwick were immensely wealthy, and their seat of power in Derbyshire was ideally situated to keep Mary Queen of Scots from court, and from the eventuality of any possible rescue by sea. Their custodianship of Mary was a coup and a show of immense favour from the English court, but it soon became clear that it was in fact a poisoned chalice. Shrewsbury himself became almost as much of a prisoner as his charge, and to make matters worse the costs of keeping Mary and her 'mock court' were astronomical. Shrewsbury was sent an allowance of £52 per week to clothe and feed them but this was later cut to just £30 a week with no real explanation possible other than Elizabeth's notorious parsimony. He frequently wrote to court begging for the correct remuneration to be considered but his pleas met with little effect.

Shrewsbury was not a harsh jailer and this possibly led to some of the later rumours that he was in fact over fond of his charge. In between plots Mary was allowed to ride, to practise archery, to watch the occasional play, and even to fraternise with some of the wealthier Derbyshire families; Shrewsbury actually got into trouble for showing her off like some sort of prize possession. For a while Mary had her own stable of horses and later on, when her health became so bad that she could barely walk, also a coach to convey her around the vast confines of Sheffield Park.

As well as needlework Mary also occupied herself with the procurement of a vast array of pets during her long imprisonment, including dogs, Skye terriers being among her favourites, and turtle doves. Although socialisation with their 'guest' was frowned upon, there was undoubtedly some cross-pollination between Mary's household and that of Shrewsbury's; on one occasion a servant from each of the respective households was dismissed because of their budding romance.

Immediately following the events of Carberry Hill, Bothwell had taken up piracy, pursued by Kirkcaldy of Grange in a daring sea chase through Shetland, which ended up with Bothwell escaping to Norway, where he was detained in the port of Bergen. A long-dead dalliance with one of his discarded mistresses, Anna Throndesen, rose up to wreck his plans when he had the astonishing misfortune to run into her not long after his arrival. He had barely settled this dispute when he was arrested on the orders of Frederick II, King of Denmark and Norway, who saw him as a valuable political pawn to be put in safekeeping until that usefulness could be utilised. Bothwell was kept as a political prisoner in much the same vein as Mary, but as his usefulness waned so the conditions of his imprisonment harshened, and he died in Dragsholm Castle, apparently chained to a pillar half his height and utterly insane.

A contemporary portrait of Mary. (Library of Congress, LC-USZ62-121212)

Several sources say that he and Mary had continued to exchange letters until his mental state collapsed. At around this time she was being shuttled forth from Sheffield Castle to the nearby Sheffield Manor Lodge, sometimes to Chatsworth, and then occasionally to Buxton, where Shrewsbury built a house especially for her so that she could take the curative spring waters. In 1578 her son James began his personal rule but showed little inclination to free his mother, fearful of spoiling his own succession chances with his godmother Elizabeth. He had the Earl of Morton executed for his role in his father's murder a couple of years later, and then endured a period of captivity of his own when he fell victim to the 'Ruthven Raid', but was soon returned to power.

INVASION OF THE JESUITS

One of the effects of the Protestant Reformation that swept across Europe was of course, logically, a Counter-Reformation. During Mary's time as a captive in England this began to be felt in more and more invasive ways, at least from the point of view of the English government. Various colleges set up to train young Catholics – Jesuits – were established across the Continent, one of the most famous of these being at Douai, organised by Cardinal William Allen. These young, zealous converts then travelled to England where they attempted to reconvert the natives. This mission was made all the more desirable in their eyes after Elizabeth I was excommunicated by Pius V. However, the excommunication also made the mission doubly dangerous, as life was made considerably more difficult for the Catholics already living in England at the time; they were made to pay heavier fines than before for refusing to attend the weekly Protestant services – 'recusancy', as it was called; those who refused to attend were 'recusants'. Among the notable Jesuits who travelled to England in the name of the Catholic cause were Robert Persons (or Parsons), who was trained at a college in Rome.

SEW ON AND SEW FORTH

Despite her pets and the occasional dalliance with horse riding and archery, the main way in which Mary most famously passed her endless years in captivity was needlework. She was already an accomplished needlewoman but up until the point of her incarceration this had been merely one of many strings to her bow, the other main passion being hunting (pun intended). The Earl of Shrewsbury's wife Bess of Hardwick was, when not building grand country houses, also an expert needlewoman and together they whiled away many a long, monotonous afternoon sewing and gossiping, often with Mary Seton in tow. Mary used many designs from pattern books for her pieces of embroidery, which she often sent away to France for; she was especially fond of sewing secret emblems and messages into her works, but she was not alone in this. The Elizabethans had a passion for secret and hidden meanings, especially in works of art. One message she sent to the Duke of Norfolk during their courtship was that of a withered vine being pruned, a reference to the barren Tudor tree of Elizabeth being cut down to make way for the far more fecund one of Mary Stuart. There was also the one of the ginger cat and the mouse, as well as various other animal emblems including a dolphin, a play on words for 'Dauphin', in memory of her first husband. Mary told a visitor to Tutbury Castle that she would often sew until the pain in her hands was so bad that she could no longer continue with the work.

In 1583 the Throckmorton Plot again put Mary centre stage. Sir Francis Walsingham by this stage had succeeded Cecil in his position when Cecil was ennobled as Lord Burghley. In 1584 Mary's presence in their household finally flung Shrewsbury and his wife Bess apart; the marriage had been all but disintegrating for years, small wonder given the woes of playing permanent hosts to the Scots queen and her mock court. Bess of Hardwick accused Mary of having an affair with her husband and even bearing him several children; Mary retaliated by sending to Elizabeth in London the notorious 'Scandal Letter', regaling her with all of the gossip

Bess had shared with her over their countless sewing bees. Burghley saw to it that the letter never reached his mistress – a mercy, given that it contained various tasty titbits concerning Elizabeth's copiously vain ego, of how Bess and Darnley's mother, the Countess of Lennox, would practically find themselves convulsed with laughter at the sight her; apparently Elizabeth believed herself to be so beautiful that it was impossible for people to look upon her queenly countenance without being dazzled. Her ladies, barely able to conceal their guffaws, clearly thought otherwise. The 'Scandal Letter' also told of Elizabeth's supposedly insatiable sexual appetite and contained the slightly more revealing comment that she 'wasn't like other women' anatomically. The sending of the letter by Mary was practically the Tudor equivalent of posting salacious snapshots of someone on their Facebook 'wall' without their consent.

Bess of Hardwick. (J.D. Leader)

Oranges Are Not the Only Fruit

As a result of the fall-out between Shrewsbury and Bess, Mary was given over to the temporary care of Sir Ralph Sadler, who had seen her as a baby when he had been Henry VIII's ambassador to Scotland. After a brief sojourn with him at Wingfield Manor she was then returned to the hated Tutbury; Mary Seton left her service at around this time, almost crippled with rheumatism from the years she had shared in captivity with her mistress. Sadler's leniency – he was prone to allowing Mary along with him on the occasional hawking expedition – not to mention his age, meant that his tenure as her custodian was mercifully brief.

Whilst Mary was in his custody the Bond of Association was drafted by Elizabeth's Privy Council. This was both a response to the fallout from the Throckmorton Plot and also a more direct response to the assassination of William of Orange, who was, next to Elizabeth herself, perhaps Europe's leading Protestant. The Bond of Association stated that any plot or attempt on Elizabeth's life, especially on behalf of another person – i.e. Mary – meant that not only the plotters but the person on whose behalf they were plotting – i.e. Mary – were to be executed, even if the person on whose behalf they were plotting was not aware of or had not even sanctioned the plot in the first place. It was basically a mandate to allow mob justice. Mary offered to sign up to the new law herself, despite the fact that it had been pretty much put into place with her in mind. Elizabeth herself was uneasy about some aspects of the new law and it required several adjustments before it was finally passed.

Toward the twilight of Mary's time with the Shrewsburys there had been several attempts to reconcile Mary to her son James, and the possibility of a joint rule had been discussed on several occasions, although the negotiations were painfully slow and protracted; this seemed to be the way that suited Elizabeth best. Scotland saw the arrival of Patrick, Master of Gray, beautiful and ruthless, who quickly ingratiated himself with the young King James. He was soon despatched to London to open negotiations with Elizabeth about both Scotland's and Mary's situation, and Mary sent her secretary Nau to monitor the proceedings. It soon became apparent that Gray was negotiating for an English alliance for Scotland that had no use or place for Mary whatsoever. Mary urged Gray to remind James of his filial duty, but the best that the beautiful young courtier could promise was to raise the issue with her son at the first available opportunity. In the end James was advised against any sort of a joint rule or association with her. All of this eventually culminated in the Treaty of Berwick, concluded in 1586 and literally days before Mary fatally – but perhaps understandably – involved herself in the final plot to free her from her long imprisonment. Elizabeth paid James a pension and the covert understanding was that he would one day succeed to her throne. There was no mention of Mary whatsoever. She blamed her son but quickly transferred those almost astonished feelings of betrayal to Gray and various other treacherous courtiers whom she believed James unwisely surrounded himself with. The fallout of the newfound fealty between her son and her jailer left her feeling utterly abandoned and essentially redundant as far as ever again becoming a reigning monarch was concerned.

Sadler was replaced as Mary's custodian by the puritan Sir Amyas Paulet, who proceeded to make Mary's life even more of a living hell than it already was, pulling down her cloth of state and censoring most of her correspondence before finally being instructed to cut it off completely. He also banished her from giving alms to the poor of Tutbury village, concerned that it was a cover by which she might win sympathy for her cause. Her laundresses seemed to cause him a great deal of consternation as well, fearful as he was that they might be smuggling secret letters amid their bundles of washing. In terms of his character Paulet seems to have reacted to Mary in much the same manner as John Knox some twenty years previously, being utterly unmoved by her beauty and if anything completely bored by her conversation. As a Puritan – the strictest sort of Protestant – he seems to have been an especially sadistic choice of gaoler for the Catholic queen. Unable to acclimatise to Tutbury's stinking drainage system, Paulet had Mary moved to the moated Chartley Manor, not far from Burton, a residence then owned by the ageing Elizabeth's notorious toy boy, the Earl of Essex. The move was made in the middle of winter – and perhaps deliberately; nothing would have been more convenient for the English court than to have their unwelcome guest perish of natural causes. Mary in fact fell so ill on her arrival that she kept to her bed for several weeks.

Anthony Babington and the Beer Barrels from Burton

It was at Chartley that Mary was first contacted by Gilbert Gifford, a Catholic double agent working for Sir Francis Walsingham. Gifford recommended to her service a young Catholic gentleman called Anthony Babington. Babington, so Gifford told her, was holding some of her waylaid correspondence and would very much like to forward it to her. Babington had once been a page in the Earl of Shrewsbury's household and may have formed a romantic attachment to the captive queen; 'calf love', as it was called in Tudor times. Via Gifford, the unwitting Babington detailed a plot to free Mary, murder Elizabeth (the wording was ambiguous but the general idea was that some accomplices of his would run her through with a sword while she was walking in the gardens at Whitehall Palace), and then set Mary on the throne with help via an invasion from Catholic Europe. The whole plot was meticulously monitored by Walsingham; in modern parlance it would most likely be called a 'sting'. The messages that passed back and forth between Mary and Babington were secreted in leather wallets which were slipped via a cork tube into the bung hole of a beer barrel. Beer had been delivered to Tutbury by the local brewer Henry Cavendish, and whilst he may have been a party to the plot that followed it seems more likely that it was the brewer at nearby Burton who was the messenger. Mary herself believed that the brewer who delivered to Chartley was working for her cause and so began replying to all of her backdated correspondence via the new channel. Beer barrels made the perfect hiding place for Mary's messages, but what she didn't know was that those messages were then passed from the brewer at Burton to Gifford, who then passed them to Walsingham's code breaker, where they were copied before being sent on to their original destinations. The brewer at Burton was therefore in the pay of both Mary – who thought that her letters were being conveyed in all honesty by him – and Paulet, on Walsingham's behalf, to ensure that the messages were given to Gifford first. Such double-dealing earned the brewer at Burton the nickname 'The Honest Man'. His real identity has long been a matter of some mystery, but there is evidence that he was one William Nicholson, who brewed his beer in the outbuildings of the former Burton Abbey; most of the buildings were at that time a manor house owned by the Catholic Sir Thomas Paget, who was known to Babington. All things were connected, one way or another.

Young, Catholic and cool; a beginner's guide to the Babington Plot

The Babington Plot, Mary's final conspiracy against Elizabeth I, is so convoluted that even today it is impossible to understand quite fully who was tricking whom, who was on what side, and so on and so forth. Separate plots to assassinate Elizabeth and free Mary were sewn together under Sir Francis Walsingham's watchful gaze, making one large terrible tapestry, one that even Mary, with her enthusiastic needle, might have wished she'd shied away from. Mary's correspondence had been cut off for almost a year by the time it began, so when her backdated mail began arriving at Chartley, with the possibility of further correspondence in a secret pipeline via the beer barrels from Burton, she naturally jumped at the chance. Via the secret pipeline her messages were sent to London to be deciphered or were even done on the spot by Phelippes, Walsingham's expert code breaker; Phelippes was secreted at Chartley for a time and had even been spotted by Mary, who rather cattily passed comment on his bad skin whilst she took the sun in her coach.

Down in London the correspondence was also coming from Anthony Babington, a well-to-do young Catholic gentleman who had been recruited by Thomas Morgan whilst in France, and who was to receive encouraging signs from eminent figures such as the former Spanish ambassador Bernardino de Mendoza; Mendoza had been involved in the Throckmorton Plot and expelled from England when his role was revealed. Thomas Morgan, like Babington, had also worked for the Earl of Shrewsbury whilst Mary and her household were in his custody. Babington brought with him his plotting pals, among them the poet Chidiock Tichbourne, John Ballard the priest, would-be assassin John Savage, and various other young disaffected – i.e. bored – Catholic gentlemen. They were foolish enough to commission a portrait of themselves for posterity, now presumed lost at the point when the plot went pear-shaped. Ballard had come over from the Continent and essentially stirred things up among them; Savage was at the spearhead of the proposed assassination plot, whose actual enactment caused the young Catholic conspirators considerable soul-searching. They had grown up in an England where Catholicism, driven underground, became something of a forbidden fruit; they were young and good-looking, and they had money. The lure of the controversial Catholic religion, combined with the seductive legend of the imprisoned Scots queen, may have fuelled their impressionable young minds. In case he wavered in his resolve Babington was poleaxed on a personal level by Robert Poley, a Catholic agent of Walsingham's, whilst Gifford encouraged the flow of counterfeit correspondence up at Chartley, eventually fleeing to the Continent when it came time to swoop on the conspirators. When Babington laid the plot before Mary, Phelippes added a postscript to her reply so that it appeared that she had asked him to name the 'six gentlemen' who were to carry out the assassination of Elizabeth. Babington and the rest of the plotters were rounded up and confessed to the entire affair. Some of them were certainly tortured, Ballard the priest so badly that he had to be carried to his execution in a chair, his limbs having been torn out of their sockets by the rack. Whilst awaiting death in the Tower of London, Chidiock Tichbourne wrote a piece of poetry that has passed down through history as 'Tichbourne's elegy', a lament on a life cut tragically short; some reports say that he read either part or all of it at his execution.

When the time came to reveal the Babington Plot, Babington himself and all his associates were arrested to great rejoicing and pealing of bells throughout the capital. Beforehand Babington had been made aware of his imminent arrest when one of Walsingham's agents invited him to dinner and accidentally left a note from his master on the table in front of him; Babington promptly scarpered to St John's Wood, but there was no escape.

THE TRIAL OF THE CENTURY

On 15 and 16 October 1586, Mary made her two appearances before the court set up to try her in the great hall of Fotheringay Castle. She was so lame she had to be aided in and out of the chamber. Elizabeth was represented by a throne, which Mary made a beeline for until being told in no uncertain terms that the smaller, more modest seat with the cushion on it was in fact reserved for her. She defended herself against Walsingham and others, denying with almost barefaced cheek any complicity in the Babington Plot and denying also that they had any jurisdiction over her, an anointed queen from a rival realm. She reminded them that she had come to England seeking help and succour from its queen but had instead suffered at that point eighteen years' imprisonment. She had no notes, and no idea of what sort of evidence they were going to produce; most of that evidence circulated around the correspondence between herself and Anthony Babington. She called Cecil her enemy and he replied with some pride that he was indeed the enemy of the enemies of Elizabeth. At one point it practically descended into a shouting match, although by the second day tempers were sufficiently calmed for normal proceedings to be resumed by both parties. Mary was curious to link faces with names and consulted Paulet frequently as to whom she was being addressed by. Among those present were the aforementioned Cecil, Walsingham, Christopher Hatton (another of Elizabeth's favourites), as well as Shrewsbury, who had pleaded beforehand to be excused the duty designated to him.

Mary's trial at Fotheringay Castle.
(BLFC, Add. 48027, f.569)

A similar fate befell Mary herself, when Paulet tricked her into embarking on a hunt near Sir Walter Aston's house at Tixall. At first she believed that the troop of horsemen riding towards her were in fact the courageous Babington plotters themselves. However, on realising the truth Mary dismounted her horse and sat on the ground, refusing to move; she then knelt under a nearby tree and prayed, as her secretaries were arrested and unceremoniously hauled away. She is said to have declared that she was no longer of any use to anyone, more than likely a direct reference to the recent amity between her son and Elizabeth, the fallout of which had probably propelled her into accepting the barely concealed lunacy of the Babington Plot in the first place. After a two-week tenure in close confinement at Tixall Hall she was returned to her ransacked rooms at Chartley and taken from thence to Fotheringay Castle in Northamptonshire for her trial. Fotheringay, the birthplace of Richard III, was now used mainly as a state prison; Mary's coachman was dismissed shortly after her arrival, leaving her perhaps in little doubt that this was to be her final stopping point on the long, weary road of captivity.

The trial reconvened in Westminster and whilst there found Mary guilty, although Elizabeth shied away from signing the death warrant for several months. She had been less squeamish when it came to Babington and his accomplices, who suffered a newly devised form of hanging, drawing and quartering; reports said that spectators were so sickened by the butchery meted out to Babington, Chidiock Tichbourne, John Ballard, John Savage and the others that Elizabeth was forced to have the second batch of plotters hanged until they were dead before being cut down and disembowelled. Savage even broke the rope when he was hung and was still alive when they cut him open. Accounts of the severity of the executions vary – as does the location, generally thought to be either St Giles or Lincoln's Inn Fields in London.

One Would Wish to Become a Martyr

Back in Fotheringay a strange sort of serenity gripped Mary Stuart as she realised that her long ordeal was soon to come to an end; she read several histories of England, parried verbally with Paulet, and began to fashion in her mind the idea that she was in fact dying as a martyr to the Catholic cause, a destiny that enabled her

Mary's execution. (Wellcome Library, London)

to endure the petty indignities her jailers heaped upon her as the winter months crept on. The fact that Elizabeth had yet to sign the death warrant gave false hope to Mary's household that perhaps she was to be shown some sort of mercy. French ambassadors petitioned Elizabeth for mercy, whilst from Scotland came several rather limp exclamations of outrage from Mary's son James.

On 1 February 1587, Elizabeth finally relented and signed Mary's death warrant, maintaining afterwards that it was then despatched without her consent; there may have been some truth in this, because Burghley and the rest of the council were so desperate to see Mary gone that they banded together and promised to back each other up in the face of their mistress's fury. Mary was told of her execution on the 7 February, amid much emotional outpouring from her servants. She stayed up for most of the night and then laid down for just a few short hours whilst fully clothed, having beforehand written out her bequests and a last letter, this one to her brother-in-law Henry III of France. She appeared in the great hall at Fotheringay on the morning of the 8th, unveiling a crimson outfit – the Catholic colour of martyrdom – and then arguing with the Protestant priest of Peterborough about his sermons before submitting herself to the axe. Shrewsbury was present, as was the Earl of Kent. Both men offered to pray with the queen but she reminded them that they were of differing religions; this was Mary's big moment and she wasn't about to have it marred by any last-minute Protestant preaching. Two of her women, Jane Kennedy and Elizabeth Curle, helped Mary with the big unveil of her crimson clothes, and there was a brief altercation between them and Bull the executioner about the ownership of Mary's crucifix; traditionally these were the spoils of the executioner. Jane Kennedy tied a white handkerchief around Mary's eyes and then departed from the small raised platform that had been erected for the occasion. Mary's hands had to be moved by Bull's assistant as she was gripping the small block with them and they would have been severed when the first blow fell. That first blow bit into the back of Mary's head and she was heard by some to exclaim out loud in shock; the second severed her head, save for one small sinew which was sawn off with the axe. Her head was lifted up by Bull and then it promptly fell away as her wig came off in his hands; Mary's short grey hair was revealed for all the world to see, even as the prayers she had been uttering continued to pass through her dead lips. The macabre scene was cemented by the sight of her little Skye terrier crawling out from under her skirts to lie piteously near her corpse. Some accounts say that her severed head was taken to one of the castle windows and waved around to the crowds gathered below, so that they could see for themselves that this grave threat to national security was now safely done away with. Her body was wrapped in the cloth from her own billiard table and then embalmed, with the vital organs being buried somewhere deep within the confines of the castle; to this day they have never been recovered. Her body remained in Fotheringay Castle until the summer, divested of the billiard cloth and sealed in a heavy lead coffin. Her servants were locked in their rooms immediately after the execution, whilst Mary's clothes and the block were burnt, to stop anyone from securing them as tangible relics to her martyrdom.

From France came a cry of national mourning for their former queen and a service was held in Notre Dame where Mary had been married so many years before; from Scotland came further limp exclamations of outrage from her son, but the common people seemed more inclined to take up the sword on their former queen's behalf than he did. When James ordered full mourning costume for his mother the Earl of Sinclair turned up clad in armour and ready for battle, declaring that what he was wearing was in fact the true mourning outfit for the Queen of Scots.

Several times Mary had apparently bequeathed her right to the English throne to Phillip II of Spain in the event that her son refused to convert to Catholicism, and a year later Phillip's Armada set sail for England in an attempt to rout the heretic Elizabeth once and for all. Before that happened Mary's servants were finally freed from

The chair at Connington church, in which Mary is believed to have sat before her execution. (BLFC, 000247776)

their confinement at Fotheringay, and slowly from their lips word of her courage at her execution spread far and wide, further fashioning the legend that Mary herself had set in motion when she had appeared in the castle's great hall on that fateful February morning.

It wasn't until the summer that Mary was actually given a proper burial, interred opposite Henry VIII's unfortunate first wife Catherine of Aragon in Peterborough Cathedral. Her body was conveyed from Fotheringay in the dead of night in a protracted and sombre procession. She was given a semblance of a full

A CHAIR FIT FOR A QUEEN

In All Saint's church, Connington, in Cambridgeshire, sits a tall, firm-backed chair, covered in cobwebs and plonked in a corner just ahead of the altar. This is said to be the chair that Mary Queen of Scots sat in shortly before she was executed, atop the small scaffold that had been erected for the occasion in the great hall of Fotheringay Castle. The church is now closed but visitors can view the chair by obtaining the key to the building from one of the locals in the nearby village; there is a sign on the door with a phone number, and the house holding the key is only a couple of streets away. The only problem with the provenance of this relic – as with many of the other items said to have been held/used/worn by Mary at her execution – is that Mary's clothes and the block on which she was executed were burnt to stop them from being obtained as relics. Whether those orchestrating her execution were thorough enough to include the chair she sat on is open to question. There is also the problem that some accounts of the execution state that it was a 'stool' that the queen sat on, although this seems unlikely for someone of her stature and in her state of health, unless it was a very tall stool indeed; more like a bar stool then, one imagines. Therefore, as with many of the items said to be associated with the legendary Mary Queen of Scots, it is best perhaps to keep an open mind, peruse the documents, and decide for yourself.

state funeral, with her remaining household still at the castle being allowed out of their confinement so that they could attend, although they withdrew from the mainly Protestant service and kept to their rooms for what would be considered the wake. Mary's body was then removed to Westminster Abbey some twenty-five years later when her son James VI succeeded to the English throne as James I of England (the site of Mary's original burial in Peterborough Cathedral is still marked). James had a magnificent monument made for Elizabeth, who was buried with her half-sister Mary on one side of the Henry VII chapel in Westminster Abbey, with a lifelike effigy on top; Mary was buried on the opposite side of the Henry VII chapel with a larger and equally lifelike effigy atop her own tomb. In this way James was seen to have gone some way to not only honouring his mother's memory but perhaps even cocking a snook at Elizabeth's, and at the role she played in Mary's death; after all, James was king now, and had no need to kowtow to the last of the Tudors.

THE MARIE STUART SOCIETY

The Marie Stuart Society was founded in 1992 to mark the 450th anniversary of the birth of Mary Queen of Scots. They have both a Scottish and an English branch and devote their time to furthering the cause of the most famous monarch in Scottish history; a number of plaques have been erected by them at various sites of Marian interest, including Dumbarton Castle, Workington, and Carberry Hill. As of this writing they are also in the process of erecting a statue to Mary at her birthplace of Linlithgow Palace. They produce a journal and undertake countless outings to sites related to Mary. As far as the Westminster Abbey memorial is concerned, they hold a service there yearly, usually on or around Mary's birthday in December, when the chapel is closed to members of the public and a small service with a flower laying is conducted; this author was privileged enough to have laid the flowers at the foot of Mary's tomb for the 2013 service.

5

Mary's Men

James IV – Mary's grandfather and one of the most successful of the Scots kings, he married Henry VIII's sister Margaret at the wishes of her father Henry VII, in an attempt to unite the two kingdoms. The peace that followed didn't last, and he was killed at the Battle of Flodden Field at the age of just forty.

James V – Mary's father, who, after a somewhat confusing and uncertain minority, went on to marry two French brides: Madeleine of Valois and then Mary's mother, Mary of Guise, pipping his uncle Henry VIII to the post where the second lady was concerned. Henry VIII had his eye on Mary of Guise as a prospective fourth wife but after he lost her to his nephew the 'honour' eventually went to the German Anne of Cleves. James V died of an apparently broken heart after the devastating Battle of Solway Moss (not so devastating that he couldn't sum things up with that tasty deathbed soundbite about the impending doom of the dynasty that his newborn daughter's birth would bring about, however). He sired numerous illegitimate children, one of whom – Moray – would cause countless troubles for his one legitimate daughter.

Henry VIII – the much-married monarch and also Mary's great-uncle, Henry VIII viewed the infant Mary Queen of Scots simply as a dynastic pawn, wanting to pluck her out of Scotland and wed her to his son.

Edward VI – the boy king who never got to meet, let alone marry Mary, but who holds the honour of being her first proper prospective bridegroom. In one of the most spectacular twists of historical irony and fate, the much anticipated boy-king of Henry VIII's dreams died a sickly fifteen-year-old, and was succeeded by one not particularly successful half-sister – 'Bloody Mary' – and then by their significantly more successful half-sister, Elizabeth I.

Edward Seymour – Edward VI's uncle, and brother to the third wife of Henry VIII, Jane Seymour; he carried on Henry's brutal retaliation against the Scots regarding the matter of Mary's marriage to his nephew until he ended up executed for treason in 1552. He was a notoriously cold fish who had thousands of Scots slaughtered just because they wouldn't hand Mary over.

Cardinal Beaton – a former ambassador to James V who had a hand in both his French marriages, David Beaton tried to become regent for Mary Queen of Scots after she was born but lost out to the 2nd Earl of Arran, James Hamilton. Beaton fell from power and the infant Mary was betrothed to Edward VI of England. When the cardinal regained his footing he saw to it that the proposed marriage was abolished, which led to further 'Rough Wooings' on the part of England. Beaton then proceeded to burn the Protestant preacher George Wishart. Various nobles took revenge by storming the castle of St Andrews and killing the cardinal, mutilating his body and hanging it from the windows. Various reports say that they urinated in the corpse's mouth, castrated him and then stuffed his own genitals in his mouth; barbarism on both sides, it must be said, given that Beaton had set himself up with a ringside seat for Wishart's burning.

2nd Earl of Arran – James Hamilton, also known as the Duke of Châtellerault, he became the rightful regent for the infant Mary after it was said that instructions left by James V to appoint Cardinal Beaton to the post had in fact been forged. Arran tended to swing both ways, in matters of religion at least. He eventually conceded the regency to Mary's mother, but was influential in having the young Queen of Scots sent to France for her wellbeing and it was for this that he earned himself the Châtellerault title.

3rd Earl of Arran – James Hamilton, son of the Duke of Châtellerault, became insane, attempting to convince both John Knox and the various lords and nobles that the Earl of Bothwell was going to kidnap Mary and marry her; this being several years before Bothwell actually *did* kidnap the queen and marry her. He was locked away from public life and lived until 1609, when all the other players in his little drama were long since dead.

Henry II of France – King of France when the young Mary went to live there, he therefore became a sort of surrogate father to her. As a young man Henry had married the Italian Catherine de Medici by arrangement but he preferred for his bed the much older but somehow eternally youthful Diane de Poiters, who was his mistress for most of his adult life and who had initially been foisted on him with a view to teaching the rather taciturn young boy the ways of the world. He died when a splinter of a lance penetrated his visor during a joust, making Mary, who had by then married his son, Queen of France. His insistence on Mary quartering her arms with those of England may have caused irreparable harm to her reputation as far as Elizabeth I and her secretary of state William Cecil were concerned.

Francis the Dauphin – Mary's first husband, and for a brief time also King of France as Francis II. Francis was sickly and sullen, but he took to Mary like a duck – or a dolphin – to water. Theirs was so much a marriage of convenience that even after their nuptials they were more like childhood playmates than passionate partners; Mary may have been still a virgin when she returned from France to Scotland after his death. His descent from the unpopular Catherine de Medici plus the fact of his ill health and resultantly bad complexion – to onlookers it seemed as though he had leprosy – meant that the French public actually grew to fear him, even going so far as to spread rumours that he drank the blood of babies in order to sate his unnatural appetites. He enjoyed hunting with a passion and left matters of statecraft more to Mary's Guise uncles, a state of affairs that seemed to suit both sides rather well. His weak constitution got the better of him and he succumbed to an ear infection not long after ascending to the throne. In the *Reign* TV series he is played by Toby Regbo.

Cardinal of Lorraine – one of Mary's uncles on her mother's side and possibly her closest advisor during her time in France; literature – and Bothwell – has, in times past, pointed out the Cardinal's relationship with his niece as being somewhat less than innocent. Certainly despite his being an intensely holy man, the cardinal of Lorraine was also an intensely amorous one, but this was nothing new for the age, when many men in the Church often had secret mistresses and sometimes children too. He ceased to be of such importance to Mary after she in her turn ceased being of such importance to the Guise family on the death of Francis, and he famously asked her to leave her jewels with him when she set sail for Scotland in case anything should happen to her on the journey; Mary famously refused to comply.

Duke of Guise – another uncle, and the second half of the 'dynamic duo' which comprised himself and the Cardinal of Lorraine, the two of them acting as Mary's chief advisors during her time in France. The Duke of Guise was a celebrated war hero who sported a battle scar on his cheek as a sign of his macho credentials which he'd picked up at the second Siege of Boulogne in 1544. He won Calais back from the English in 1558, a massive coup for an already glorious military career, but was assassinated in 1563; together with his younger brother the Cardinal of Lorraine the two men were the most significant influence on Mary during her childhood in France, working for their interests and that of the Guise dynasty as much as they were working for her own. It has been said that Mary may have viewed the battle-scarred Duke of Guise as the ideal image of manhood, which fits well with her purported predilection for the equally tough Bothwell, but less so with her desire for the rather more demure Darnley.

Earl of Moray – Mary's half-brother, and certainly the biggest Scottish thorn in her side despite an initial pretence of filial friendship. Moray was one of James V's many illegitimate children and therefore was barred from taking the throne, although he settled in the end for the regency, which was to him the next best thing, at least until someone put a bullet through his head for being such a despot. His logic in bringing a young, vibrant, attractive Mary back to Scotland a) when he wanted the reins of power for himself anyway and b) considering that it had just ceased to be a Catholic country, leaves one wondering exactly how much political acumen he really possessed. When Mary was deposed he gave much of her confiscated jewellery to his wife, Lady Agnes Keith. He is buried today in St Giles' Cathedral on Edinburgh's Royal Mile. Onscreen perhaps his best-known portrayal is by the actor Patrick 'The Prisoner' McGoohan in the 1971 movie *Mary, Queen of Scots*.

Earl of Moray.
(BLFC, 003317067)

Charles IX – Francis the Dauphin's younger brother, Charles succeeded him to the throne on the boy-king's death. He was rather taken with Mary himself and wanted to marry her when he came to the throne, but Catherine de Medici was having none of it; apparently she'd never gotten over Mary having disparagingly referred to

Henry III of Valois.
(BLFC, 001833946)

her as 'a merchant's daughter', which in effect she was. Charles was rather a bad-tempered boy and never much more than a puppet king for his far more commanding – not to mention cunning – mother. He presided over the wars of religion which were to ravage France during much of his reign, culminating in the Massacre of St Bartholomew's Eve, and he died shortly thereafter, probably from tuberculosis. He was succeeded by his brother Henry III.

Nicholas Throckmorton – English ambassador who first met Mary whilst she was Queen of France, Throckmorton spent most of his time there trying to get her to ratify the Treaty of Edinburgh, but without much success. Despite this, and despite being a devout Protestant with an intense dislike of the Guises, he seemed to be one of the many men who fell under the fascination that Mary exerted. The feeling seemed to be somewhat mutual as Mary was enamoured enough of Throckmorton to send his wife Lady Throckmorton a series of gilt gifts. Throckmorton was sent to Scotland to plead Mary's case in the aftermath of the Battle of Carberry Hill, and attempted to send messages to her whilst she was a prisoner on Lochleven; he fell from favour after being involved in the 'Rising of the North', and his nephew later caused trouble for Elizabeth via Mary in the Throckmorton Plot. Nicholas Throckmorton's daughter Bess would in time be a lady-in-waiting to Elizabeth, causing scandal by secretly marrying one of her favourites, the dashing explorer Sir Walter Raleigh.

Sir William Cecil (later Lord Burghley) – Elizabeth I's chief advisor, secretary of state, and without doubt Mary's arch-enemy. As someone who had lived through the horrors of Elizabeth's half-sister's reign, he probably thought his fears regarding another Catholic queen were well founded, although Mary Queen of Scots was famously tolerant and not at all partial to putting heretics to the faggot. Cecil made it his life's work to destabilise her rule and saw his task through to the bitter end by having her death warrant despatched without Elizabeth's consent. He was ennobled as Lord Burghley in later life and is sometimes referred to as such.

Such was Elizabeth's affection for him that she is said to have spoon-fed him with her own hand as he lay on his deathbed. For those supporters of Mary who want to stand and cock a snook at his rather elaborate tomb, he is buried in St Martin's church, Stamford (not far from the rather magnificent Burghley House).

William Cecil, later Lord Burghley.
(Wellcome Library, London)

George Buchanan – a Scottish scholar, poet and humanist who revered Mary and read prose and poetry with her until she got mixed up with Bothwell, at which point he performed one of the more melodramatic about-turns of her entire supporting cast, from which point on he instead penned various diatribes against her, as well as cuffing her poor son around the back of the head on a frequent basis once he became his teacher.

John Leslie, Bishop of Ross – one-time ambassador of Mary's and one of her staunchest supporters, Leslie was at Mary's side as far back as her time in France, when, as a staunch Catholic, he strongly advised her to take Scotland back by storm if needs be. His nerve gave way when dangled in front of the rack during the Ridolfi Plot, and he spent the rest of his queen's captivity plotting on her behalf from the safer vantage point of the Continent.

Thomas Randolph – Elizabeth's ambassador to Mary's court during the early to middle part of her Scottish reign; he courted Mary Beaton, one of her Four Maries, but his plan to have her spy on her royal mistress put the kibosh on the romance when she pointedly refused. He was expelled from the country for refusing to toe the line when it came to Mary's marriage to Darnley, but was back in Scotland to see their son James VI when he took control of his destiny in the late 1570s.

John Knox – Scottish Protestant preacher par excellence, and a man able to reduce Mary to tears with the sort of tongue-lashing that really ought to have seen his head neatly disengaged from his shoulders. He was one of the leading lights of the Scottish Reformation, with a chip on his shoulder as a result of having done time on the French slave galleys after his involvement in the assassination of Cardinal Beaton. Whilst in Europe the already ardent Protestant became what would be considered in modern terms 'radicalised'. Knox carried on as though he had a personal hotline to God, but despite his holier-than-thou demeanour he had a propensity for teen brides and besides that a beard almost as long as his legs. Rather fittingly for someone who was so unbelievably disrespectful to Mary, the site of his grave is now in the car park of St Giles' Cathedral on the Royal Mile in Edinburgh; one imagines Mary would have been highly amused to know that so many old bangers were parked atop his belligerent bones. Nevertheless he is revered as something of a national hero in Scotland and his few meetings with Mary are the subject of countless paintings and postcards. Also on the Royal Mile and well worth a visit is John Knox House, where he is said to have lived toward the end of his life, and which houses an extensive exhibition on the man and his morals. There are impressive statues of John Knox in Geneva, Glasgow, and of course Edinburgh.

Maitland of Lethington – as Sir William Cecil was to Elizabeth I, so William Maitland of Lethington was to Mary, bagging one of her Four Maries – Mary Fleming – in the bargain. He had also worked for Mary of Guise but betrayed her when the religious situation in Scotland reached breaking point, a fact of which Mary Queen of Scots reminded him when she returned from France. An astute politician whose loyalty was perhaps more to the idea of a Scotland united with England than to his sovereign, Maitland conducted a long, arduous campaign to secure Mary her rights of succession. He switched sides during the bother with Bothwell but switched back again in time to die mysteriously – suicide has been speculated – whilst helping hold Edinburgh Castle for her during her captivity; he is buried in Haddington, presumably with his wife alongside him. Maitland met Elizabeth I on several occasions during the discussions over Mary's right to succeed her, and also Mary's early marriage negotiations, and corresponded frequently with Cecil throughout. How much Maitland – and perhaps even Cecil – was involved in both the Rizzio and the Darnley murders remains something of a mystery. By the time Mary

Maitland of Lethington.
(BLFC, 003855677)

was a captive in England Maitland had, as said, changed sides and was again supporting her, at which time he also mooted a possible marriage for her with the Duke of Norfolk. Maitland is the star of Reay Tannahill's novel *Fatal Majesty*, concerning Mary's short personal tenure on the Scottish throne; think the Scottish version of Hilary Mantel's *Wolf Hall*.

James Melville – Mary's ambassador to England, whose memoirs of his meetings with Elizabeth set the scene for some of the more farcical aspects of the rivalry between the two queens; Elizabeth grilled him on Mary's height, appearance, aptitude at dancing and skill at playing the virginals, staging a scene the next night when he stumbled across her playing on her own set of the instrument, whereupon she faked surprise at having been discovered at her music; the phrase 'camp contrivance' springs to mind. Melville was one of the few courtiers with Mary when she was said to have been abducted by Bothwell and he testified that the earl raped her when they reached Dunbar Castle; his memoirs are responsible for shedding light on many of the incidents during Mary's reign, although they were written many years after the fact, and are lathered with self-congratulatory bias.

Robert Dudley (later Earl of Leicester) – the alleged love of Elizabeth's life, but a love she was willing to bargain away by sending him to Mary to marry, perhaps so that she could keep an eye on the Scots queen or also – equally as likely – so that said Scots queen wouldn't marry someone who might then encourage her to turn on Elizabeth and try to take the throne of England for herself. Dudley ended up keeping his feet firmly in England but may have crossed paths with Mary whilst they were both taking the waters at Buxton.

Chastelard – a French poet who accompanied Mary on her return to her homeland; he became so enamoured with her that he took to hiding under her bed, and ended up being executed for his troubles. Chastelard was either a Stewart stalker or someone determined to blemish Mary's reputation on behalf of French Huguenots/Protestants. Mary Fleming shared her mistress's bed afterwards, just in case there were any copycats capering about the halls of Holyrood Palace.

Earl of Lennox – Darnley's dad, who became regent after Moray was assassinated; a high-risk job, because he soon ended up dead as well. The famous 'Darnley Jewel', which is on display in Holyrood Palace, may have been made for him by his wife, Margaret Douglas. Lennox was a Scot who defected to England and married Henry VIII's niece, the aforementioned Margaret. He never forgave his daughter-in-law Mary for her alleged involvement in his son's death whereas Darnley's mother eventually did.

David Rizzio – Mary's Italian secretary and the subject of one of the most famous murders in Scottish history; in appearance he was – according to various sources and portraits – either utterly hideous or a bit of a beauty. Certainly his company was congenial enough for Mary to stay up all hours of the night playing cards with him, and it wasn't long before he was seen lounging around Holyrood Palace wearing the latest French and Italian fashions.

For this – and perhaps because people thought he was a papal spy – Rizzio was dragged from her supper chamber and butchered in front of Mary's eyes by her disgruntled husband and various Scottish lords. His grave is either in the grounds of the Canongate Kirk on Edinburgh's Royal Mile or somewhere close by Holyrood Abbey (unmarked). Perhaps the most famous of all the people to have played Rizzio onscreen is Ian *'Lord of the Rings'* Holm in the Vanessa Redgrave *Mary, Queen of Scots* movie in 1971.

Darnley – Mary's second husband; a vain, beautiful beast of a boy who put on a good show of manners until he had the crown matrimonial in his sights. Darnley was of roughly the same descent as Mary on the English side, not to mention also having Scottish descent through his father, and had been groomed for a great destiny by his pushy parents from an early age. He helped orchestrate Rizzio's murder partly in order to get the crown matrimonial and also because he was jealous of the fact that Mary stayed up until all hours playing cards with the little Italian. He turned traitor against his fellow nobles when Mary managed to convince him he was next on their list, all as part of her bid to escape from the sudden and violent coup following Rizzio's murder. Despite this Darnley then ended up the subject himself of *another* of the most famous murders in Scottish history, narrowly avoiding being blown to smithereens in Kirk O'Field, only to be discovered and suffocated as he escaped the gunpowder. Although he was buried in Holyrood Abbey, his bones were desecrated sometime during the Civil War and a few of them even turned up on sale through various reputable outlets. What may be his skull is on display in the Royal College of Surgeons, and it apparently has all the signs of belonging to someone who was syphilitic. Former 007 Timothy Dalton is perhaps the most famous actor to have played him, again in the 1971 Vanessa Redgrave movie.

3rd Lord Ruthven – sinister Scots sorcerer who headed Rizzio's assassination and died in exile a few months later, apparently convinced he was being carried off to Heaven by a flock of grateful angels. He appeared in the doorway to the supper room at Holyrood Palace on the night of the famous murder in full armour; in sixteenth-century Scotland apparently even a slaying was worth getting dressed up for.

Bothwell – Mary's third husband and, depending on whether you read romantic fiction or hardcore history, either the hunky hero of the borders who swept the Scots queen off her feet in a whirlwind romance, or a rough-edged rapist and opportunist who set his sights on her purely as a path to the crown. Despite his less than salubrious reputation, it is worth noting that he was in fact fairly well educated – even highly educated – for his time, having studied in France, which was the fashion for the nobility of Scotland. Bothwell ended his days in a Danish jail, his mummified head frequently used as a football by local kids in subsequent centuries. That jail – Dragsholm – is now a hotel of all things, and naturally his ghost is said to haunt its corridors …

Morton – another sinister Scots noble, James Douglas, 4th Earl of Morton was involved up to his elbows in both the Rizzio and the Darnley murders and still managed to secure the regency for himself after Darnley's dad Lennox died; Darnley's son got him in the end though, when James VI/I had him executed for his father's murder on one of the maiden voyages of the innovative new guillotine known as the Maiden. Morton was perhaps the most loathsome of all of Mary's backstabbing Scots lords, leading the taunts tossed up to the queen while she in turn flung rather more decorous put-downs from the safety of the battlements at Borthwick Castle, all the way through to egging on Patrick, Lord Lindsay to engage Bothwell in single combat on Carberry Hill a couple of days later.

James VI/I – Mary's son and not quite the repository of filial affection that she would have liked to believe. James was more interested in securing his succession rights to the English throne than he was with freeing his mother from her interminable captivity, despite getting a dose of it himself via the 'Ruthven Raid'. He possessed neither the height nor the stunning looks of either of his parents, having a rather awkward gait and sad, sunken eyes. He succeeded to the throne of England in 1603 alongside his wife Anne of Denmark, despite having a predilection for handsome young male courtiers. In a moment of supreme irony he almost went the same way as his father in the Gunpowder Plot of 1605. He is perhaps best remembered today for giving the country the King James Bible.

Mary's son, James VI/I.
(Wellcome Library, London)

Huntly – the first Huntly whose story matters in this narrative was George Gordon, whilst the second Huntly attached to Mary's tale was Bothwell's brother-in-law and the son of the said George Gordon. The elder Gordon's abortive coup against Mary in 1562 saw his corpse held for trial as a result of his rebellion. This was the rather 'quaint' custom of the day; historical records fail to elaborate on whether someone actually stood with their hand alongside the corpse's jaw in order to move it up and down in response to the accusations. The elder Huntly was one of the most powerful Catholic lords but went down because Mary's half-brother Moray wanted the titles his family held, and also because Mary had to be seen to be impartial when it came to calming her bothersome nobles, even where a religious ally was concerned. The younger Huntly was restored to his father's titles and became Bothwell's brother-in-law when his sister Jean Gordon married the swaggering borderer.

The Balfour brothers – owners of Kirk O'Field and possible authors of the Casket Letters; James Balfour had actually been Mary's secretary for a time, before she decided that she preferred amusing little Italians to pen her missives instead. James Balfour turned traitor and lured Mary and Bothwell into a trap by assuring them that Edinburgh Castle was at their disposal when in fact it was anything but.

'French Paris' – one of Bothwell's body servants, a young man whose sooty face was said to have so alarmed Mary when she emerged from Kirk O'Field on the night of the explosion, not long before the blast actually occurred, that she asked him why he was so grubby; he paid for his crime, as did most of his master's men, with torture and eventual execution.

Du Croc – French ambassador who tried to broker peace between the warring factions at Carberry Hill.

Kirkcaldy of Grange – fearsome but honourable Scots warrior who fought at Carberry Hill and led Mary by the reins of her horse into the waiting mob; he also fought against her at Langside but later switched sides and held Edinburgh Castle for her along with Maitland, and was executed for his troubles; there is a plaque to him at Edinburgh Castle just inside the path leading up to the castle from the main gateway/ticket office.

4th Lord Ruthven/Earl of Gowrie – son of the sinister sorcerer who headed the murder of Rizzio, the younger Ruthven fell for Mary's charms whilst she was imprisoned on Lochleven and was booted off the island as a result. He later became the Earl of Gowrie and gained possession of the Casket Letters after they were returned to Scotland following the commission into Mary's conduct held at York. He later orchestrated the 'Raid of Ruthven' whereby the young king James VI was kidnapped. Eventually James escaped and Gowrie was executed, and from thence it is generally believed that the Casket Letters came into the hands of the young king, who probably had them destroyed.

William Douglas – Moray's half-brother and the keeper of Lochleven Castle when Mary was imprisoned there. When Mary escaped he tried to stab himself as a way of saying sorry but wasn't apparently very successful. The castle fell into disuse shortly afterwards.

'Pretty Geordie' Douglas – another half-brother of the Earl of Moray, and a bit of a pin-up by all accounts; Geordie joined the queue forming behind the younger Ruthven in vying for Mary's affections whilst she was on Lochleven and helped to orchestrate her eventual escape; he remained with her during some of her captivity but the exact duration is unknown, as is that of …

Willie Douglas – supposedly an illegitimate son of William Douglas of Lochleven, 'little Willie' also had a hand in Mary's escape from Lochleven. What may have been the keys he stole to lock the gates behind them were recovered centuries later and recently displayed in Edinburgh in the National Museum of Scotland as part of their massive Mary Queen of Scots exhibition. He 'served time' with Mary whilst she was in England and seems to have left her service after the ructions caused by the Ridolfi Plot; nevertheless he remained in her thoughts sufficiently for Mary to mention him in the bequests she made at Fotheringay shortly before her execution.

Patrick, Lord Lindsay – Mary's half-brother Moray aside, it is hard to choose the most unpleasant of Mary's many backstabbing Scots lords, but whilst it may be Morton who wins the prize, Patrick, Lord Lindsay certainly comes in a close second. He was at the head of the mob which decided to mess with Mary's initial Mass at Holyrood, and also involved in the murder of Rizzio. When Mary confronted her rebellious lords at Carberry Hill, it was Lindsay who came closest to slugging it out with Bothwell in combat, wielding the legendary two-handed sword of Morton's ancestor, Archibald Bell-the-Cat. Lindsay's nadir of nastiness was achieved when he threatened to slit

Mary's throat – or cut her into pieces and cast her into the lake; accounts vary – when she was forced to abdicate whilst being kept prisoner on Lochleven.

Sir Francis Knollys – Mary's first custodian, appointed after she initially arrived in England and was housed at Carlisle Castle. Knollys had married Catherine Carey, Mary Boleyn's daughter, so he was considered 'family' by Elizabeth I. Knollys was impressed by Mary's courage and wit and also by the way Mary Seton was able to style her hair differently on a daily basis. He became less enamoured of his charge when his wife passed away whilst he was still on duty attending to the Scots queen at Bolton Castle, after Elizabeth I prevented him from returning to London to attend to her.

Lord Scrope – co-custodian of Mary at Carlisle, he later played a more prominent role when she was moved to his own residence of Bolton Castle. His wife was pregnant at the time and struck up something of a friendship with Mary; her brother was the Duke of Norfolk, so she most likely had matchmaking in mind.

6th Earl of Shrewsbury – George Talbot is possibly the man who could lay claim to having spent more time in Mary's company than any other, and whether she liked it or not. He was her custodian/jailer from January 1569 until August 1584, and because of her importance as a state prisoner was therefore essentially almost as much of a captive as she was. Elizabeth would rant and rail if Shrewsbury so much as dared stay away from his charge for more than a night or two, despite the garrison he left to guard her, not to mention his wife, termagant par excellence Bess of Hardwick. Shrewsbury owned most of Derbyshire and was well suited financially to house the Queen of Scots and her mock court, but he never received the correct financial remuneration he was due for his somewhat thankless task, and Mary's retinue, not to mention her expensive habit of bathing in white wine, almost bankrupted him. A bit like Bothwell, he has been charged in romantic novels with falling for Mary, and it was this accusation that led to the breakdown of his marriage, so there may be a kernel of truth to it; some of these novels, particularly Philippa Gregory's *The Other Queen*, even give Mary a touch of 'Stockholm syndrome' and suggest that she might have become emotionally attached to her custodian. He has a magnificent tomb in Sheffield Cathedral, well away from his wife Bess, who is in Derby Cathedral; possibly not far enough, the two of them would conclude.

Huntingdon – rival claimant to the English throne who assisted Shrewsbury with the custody of Mary during the 'Rising of the North'; Mary was always petrified about being removed into his custody on a permanent basis in case he did away with her on the quiet.

Westmorland – one of the two Northern Earls who orchestrated the 'Rising of the North'; he managed to escape to the Continent but never saw his wife and children again.

Northumberland – the other of the two earls who orchestrated said 'Rising of the North'; he escaped to Scotland but was betrayed and handed over to Elizabeth and summarily executed.

Thomas Howard, 4th Duke of Norfolk – prospective candidate for Mary's fourth husband who got his head chopped off for becoming too entangled in the plots to free her; Howard had been up until that point the premier nobleman in England. His sister was Lady Scrope of Bolton Castle, who may have had a hand in organising the match. He is played by ninth *Doctor Who* Christopher Eccleston in the first of the two Cate Blanchett Elizabeth I movies, *Elizabeth* (1998), but the onscreen chronology is completely out of kilter as he dies years before he even meets Mary.

Sir Francis Walsingham – the man who brought about Mary's downfall, Walsingham was Elizabeth's spymaster and the arch-enemy of all things Catholic. He funded his spy network out of his own pocket, knowing this was the best way to go about things rather than petitioning for funds from his notoriously parsimonious mistress. How much of the Babington Plot was a 'honey trap' partially concocted by Walsingham is a matter of great historical debate. He has been played onscreen by Geoffrey Rush (*Elizabeth* and *Elizabeth – The Golden Age*), and Patrick Malahide (*Elizabeth I*), among others.

Sir Francis Walsingham, the man who brought down Mary Queen of Scots. (Wellcome Library, London)

POPED IN, SOULED OUT

As a Catholic queen Mary's loyalty would always be to the head of the Holy Roman Church – or 'Kirk', as the Scots called it – in Rome, and that head was the Pope himself. During Mary's lifetime there were eight Popes: Paul III (1534–1549); Julius III (1550–1555); Marcellus II (1555); Paul IV (1555–1559); Pius IV (1559–1565); Pius V (1566–1572); Gregory XIII (1572–1585); and Sixtus V (1585–1590). The earlier Popes played little part in Mary's life but when in 1570 Pius V excommunicated Elizabeth I – whilst Mary was her captive – their actions began to have serious ramifications for her life in a rather more direct way. Pius V also gave his backing to the Ridolfi Plot, conspiring with Phillip II for the planned invasion of England. When sentence of death was passed on Mary in the aftermath of the Babington Plot, Mary wrote to the-then Pope Sixtus V begging for her life. This letter is preserved in the Vatican archives.

The Rollestons – father and son who were among those who attempted to rescue Mary whilst she was at Chatsworth; they and several others were either executed or imprisoned for their troubles.

Roberto Ridolfi – author of the infamous Ridolfi Plot, this Florentine banker was behind perhaps the biggest attempt to prise Mary out of captivity and place her on the throne, with the Duke of Norfolk as her prospective husband. His extensive travels did much to publicise the plot with the Pope and various others, but there was little in the way of actual support and he vastly overestimated the backing of English Catholics for the endeavour. Despite this he actually managed to make a clean getaway when the whole thing was uncovered by Cecil and his secret spy service. Francis Edwards hypothesised that Ridolfi may in fact have been working for Cecil and Walsingham the whole time, in an early Babington Plot-style sting, with the intention of dragging Mary's name even further into the mud.

Don Jon of Austria – another potential bridegroom for the captive Queen of Scots, he was the illegitimate half-brother of Phillip of Spain and a famous war hero, who unfortunately succumbed to typhoid before he could liberate Mary from the confines of Sheffield Castle.

Phillip II – Elizabeth I's brother-in-law by his marriage to her half-sister 'Bloody Mary', he plotted and planned against Elizabeth for decades before finally launching the Spanish Armada against her in 1588, an action which may in part have been pushed forward in retaliation for Mary's execution. Mary repeatedly wrote to him for help during her captivity whilst he in response dragged his heels on doing anything about it on an epic scale, making him almost as much of a procrastinator as his stingy sister-in-law.

William Parry – demented doctor who plotted to run Elizabeth through with a sword or alternatively to shoot her – accounts vary of the so-called 'Parry Plot' of 1584 – and of whose plotting Mary insisted she had no knowledge whatsoever, despite the fact that Parry had in France been heavily acquainted with one of her servants, Thomas Morgan; Morgan had worked for Shrewsbury whilst Mary was in his custody, when he became one of Mary's many adherents.

Esme Stewart – son of the regent Lennox's brother. Esme was a handsome hunk and therefore an instant hit with the young James VI/I, helping galvanise plots to have the young king's mother moved from her imprisonment. The 'Ruthven Raid', orchestrated by the Earl of Gowrie, put paid to his plans and he was forced to return to France, where he died. Whilst he was high in favour with the impressionable young James, Esme was elevated to the titles of Earl and then Duke of Lennox and also gained a place on the king's Privy Council.

Francis Throckmorton – a nephew of Sir Nicholas Throckmorton, Francis was behind some of the 1583 Throckmorton Plot to free Mary, picking up correspondence for her that had been deposited at the French Embassy just off Fleet Street in London. The discovery of the plot by Sir Francis Walsingham in turn led to a much stricter confinement for the Queen of Scots and also led to the creation of the Bond of Association, whereby English subjects were asked to put their names to a law to do away with anyone – i.e. Mary – attempting to overthrow Elizabeth's rule, even if they were not aware of the plot in the first place. Francis Throckmorton held out under several gruelling sessions on the rack before his nerve – along with most of his tendons – snapped and he told them everything. Mary herself offered to sign the Bond of Association but she wasn't fooling anyone.

Patrick, Master of Gray – as much of a chameleon when it came to religion as Darnley, Patrick was by all accounts an impossibly beautiful young man who naturally found himself in the good graces of the young King James VI/I during the twilight years of Mary's long imprisonment. He helped broker the deal that kept Mary locked up and secured the treaty between James and

Elizabeth that unofficially saw the English queen all but recognise him as her heir. He fell from grace with James because of his double-dealing but soon found himself restored to favour, perhaps courtesy of those aforementioned angelic looks. Those looks were such that they may even have inspired the Scottish historian and novelist Nigel Tranter to write a series of books about him, the *Master of Gray Trilogy*.

Sir Ralph Sadler – English ambassador of such longevity that he could lay claim to having cradled the infant Mary Queen of Scots in his arms at Linlithgow Palace, and then some forty-three years later played the role of custodian after she was removed from Shrewsbury's care and taken to Wingfield Manor. Too lenient for his own good, Sadler petitioned to be removed from the post as soon as possible.

Sir Amyas Paulet – a strict Puritan and Mary's final custodian, he found her constant declarations of innocence tedious and tore down her cloth of state to make his point; Mary, in return, thought him one of the oddest men she had ever come across. Despite being such a tinpot tyrant, he did however refuse to act as a private assassin for Elizabeth and do away with Mary so that the English queen wouldn't have to soil her hands with a public execution. Hamilton Dyce does a fantastic turn as Paulet in the 'Horrible Conspiracies' episode of the 1971 BBC series *Elizabeth R*.

Nau and Curll (or Curle) – Mary's main secretaries during her captivity, Nau was French whilst Curll was a Scotsman. They were the ones responsible for penning her reply to Babington, under her strict supervision, of course. They were both arrested when the whole plot fell apart and Mary never saw them again. Curll was imprisoned for over a year but Nau was sent back to France with a nice little windfall, which has led to some suggestion that his loyalties might not have been altogether honest. Despite this we do have Nau to thank for the dictation he took down regarding Mary's life and times, which he wrote up dutifully for her whilst sharing her long captivity.

Thomas Phelippes – Walsingham's pockmarked pocket plotter, Phelippes was a master code-breaker who may or may not have inserted incriminating sentences into Mary's reply to Babington endorsing his plot to free her and assassinate Elizabeth. He almost definitely *did* ask for the names of the 'six gentlemen' who were to assassinate Elizabeth, and also drew a gallows on the outside of the letter to signify his success in ensnaring the Queen of Scots.

Anthony Babington – Anthony Babington of Dethick Manor Farm may have become enamoured of Mary when he served as a page in Shrewsbury's household; a walnut tree said to have grown from a seed he dropped from his pocket now stands tall and twisted in the ruins of Wingfield Manor. He was eviscerated for his troubles in trying to free Mary from Chartley, as were all his compatriots, including the young gentleman who helped pen his replies to the captive queen, Chidiock Tichbourne; Tichbourne composed a touching elegy on the perils of aiding maligned monarchs from his cell in the Tower of London.

6

Mary's Maids

Margaret Tudor – Mary's grandmother and mother of James V, she was also Henry VIII's sister. Margaret married James IV in an attempt by her father, Henry VII, to unite the two warring kingdoms, Margaret having been sent to Scotland as James's prospective bride when she was little more than a child. After her husband was killed in the Battle of Flodden Field in 1513 she married Archibald Douglas, although the marriage ended acrimoniously; by him she had Margaret Douglas, Darnley's mother. Her relations with her brother in England were at best cordial and at worst downright hostile, with Henry always seeming to have preferred his younger sister, Mary.

Mary of Guise – Mary's mother, and a scion of the powerful Guise family in France. Her first marriage was to Louis II d'Orléans, the Duke of Longueville, but she was widowed at the age of just 21. She went to Scotland to marry James V after his first wife Madeleine died and once there bore him several sons, both of whom died in infancy. She had left her son from her first marriage behind in France in order to go ahead with the arranged marriage with the King of Scots. Mary then gave birth to Mary Queen of Scots in 1542 but James V died shortly after, either worn out or ravaged with illness due to the 'Rough Wooings'; probably a combination of both. Mary of Guise sent her daughter to France for safekeeping when the grasping English got too close for comfort. She became regent of Scotland in 1554 and spent the few subsequent years left to her trying to stem the tide of the Reformation, but without resorting to the small-scale genocide employed by Mary Tudor in England. Mary of Guise eventually died of dropsy in Edinburgh Castle, worn down by the religious strife then threatening to tear the country apart; Fanny Ardant plays her to fantastic effect in the first of the Cate Blanchett Elizabeth I films, *Elizabeth*. Francis, the son she left behind in France, died during the visit paid by Mary of Guise to her daughter.

Mary Fleming* – one of Mary Queen of Scots' famous 'Four Maries', she eventually married Mary's secretary Maitland of Lethington and is rumoured to be buried alongside him in Haddington. Mary Fleming shared Mary's bed for many years after the Chastelard stalker incident, and was chosen to be 'Queen of the Bean' on Twelfth Night of 1564, a tradition whereby, as the 12 Days of Christmas are concluded, on Twelfth Night a cake is cooked with a bean hidden inside; whoever finds the bean is queen for the rest of that evening. Mary Fleming was by all accounts revealed to be a bit of a babe when fitted out in her 'bean queen' outfit made up mainly of borrowed royal bling. Mary Fleming's marriage to the much older Maitland gave her children whom she brought up in the Catholic faith, a risky proposition in the Scotland into which they were born; their son James turned out to be a bit of a disappointment, though. When Maitland died and his body was to be desecrated, as was the fate of all traitors, Mary Fleming wrote to Elizabeth I personally, the Queen of England intervening on her behalf with the then regent Morton to see that he was instead given a decent burial.

Mary Beaton* – another of Mary Queen of Scots' famous 'Four Maries', Mary Beaton was perhaps the most beautiful of them all, beautiful enough for the poet George Buchanan to dedicate one of his verses to her, and certainly beautiful enough for the English ambassador Randolph to fall for her; she is said to have reciprocated, but baulked at being a spy for him. Her aunt Janet –

rumoured to be a witch – was one of Bothwell's many lovers and is said to have taught him 'the black arts'. How Mary Beaton departed company from the queen and what became of her is something of a mystery, but the parting was said to have been somewhat acrimonious and to be concerned with the matter of ownership of some jewellery. She married Alexander Ogilvy of Boyne and by him had one son. It has been postulated that perhaps Mary Beaton, whose handwriting most closely resembled the queen's, was in fact the author of the various interpolated passages of the Casket Letters. The fact that they perhaps parted acrimoniously lends weight to this assertion. If that is the case it must also be considered that Beaton may have been forced into the forgery against her will; having threatened to cut the queen up and toss her into Lochleven lake if she refused to abdicate, it is hardly likely that the new regime would baulk at threatening to dish out a similar sort of fate to one of her women.

Mary Seton* – yet another of Mary Queen of Scots' famous 'Four Maries', Mary Seton took a vow of chastity at some point during her formative years and remained unmarried for the rest of her life, although at one point she did almost marry Mary's master of the household Andrew Beaton, but he died. Mary Seton endured seventeen years of her mistress's captivity before ill health forced Mary Queen of Scots to send her to the Convent of Saint-Pierre in Rheims; the abbess was the queen's aunt and the sister of Mary of Guise. Mary Seton died there in ill health and poverty in 1615.

Mary Livingston* – the last of Mary Queen of Scots' famous 'Four Maries', Mary Livingston married John Sempill, a son of Lord Sempill; the family continued to support Mary after she fled from Scotland. Mary Livingston was responsible for the care of the queen's jewellery. Out of all the Four Maries she particularly aroused the fanatical ire of John Knox, who seemed utterly scandalised by the fact that a happy young girl would like to pass her evenings in energetic dancing and song, although his accusations that she was pregnant out of wedlock were way off the mark.

* THE FOUR MARIES

The 'Four Maries' – Mary Fleming, Mary Beaton, Mary Seton, and Mary Livingston – made up Mary Queen of Scots' famous 'Four Maries', a group of ladies-in-waiting who went to France with the queen when they were children and then served her for various tenures throughout their adult lives. As well as a plaque at Seagate Castle in North Ayrshire commemorating their visit, the Four Maries even have a pub named after them in Mary's birthplace of Linlithgow, just across the road from Linlithgow Palace itself. There's also a sonnet said to be about them, although it goes awry with the last line:

Last night there were four Marys;
Tonight there'll be but three:
There was Mary Beaton and Mary Seton
And Mary Carmichael and Me.

There was no 'Mary Carmichael' involved with Mary Queen of Scots as far as the records show, and it may be that this sonnet in fact refers to the ladies-in-waiting of Catherine I of Russia, although the fact that she also had ladies called 'Seton' and 'Beaton' is quite the coincidence. The Four Maries may also be the 'pretty maids all in a row' of the nursery rhyme 'Mary, Mary, Quite Contrary', but again this has been disputed and the true origins of it are lost in the mists of time. The faithful Mary Seton was the longest lived of the 'Four Maries', and all of them have appeared numerous times in fiction and in various film and TV depictions; the best is the Katharine Hepburn *Mary of Scotland*, where they actually get a little screen time all of their own.

Antoinette of Guise – a formidable matriarch and Mary's maternal grandmother, who wrote to the young princess's mother on her arrival in France to tell her how impressed and taken the French court was with her.

Catherine de Medici – wife of Henry II of France, described as 'the Italian woman' (one isn't entirely sure whether this was a compliment or in fact some sort of slur), she was relegated to the background during most of her husband's marriage by his obsession for his mistress, Diane de Poiters. Mary is said to have referred to her rather disparagingly as 'a merchant's daughter', which in a sense she was, although Catherine's family effectively ruled her native Florence and she was related to the Pope, who was her father's uncle. She became queen mother on the death of her husband, and regent for her son Charles IX on the death of Mary's first husband, her eldest son Francis (Francis II). Catherine consulted astrologers, Nostradamus among them, supposedly resorted to sorcery in an effort to get pregnant, and apparently had a penchant for poisoning people who got in her way; one of her most famous 'crimes' was getting rid of her prospective husband's brother so that he could become king in his stead. The cup-bearer who had brought the alleged poison to the-then king's lips was tied

Catherine de Medici, Mary's first mother-in-law. (BLFC, 001833946)

down and had each of his limbs attached to a horse. The horses were started by some loud noise and galloped off, each taking one of said limbs of the cup-bearer with them. On top of that she also had a hole drilled in the floor of her apartments, situated above her husband's, so that she could spy on him and Diane when they were making love. Despite these decidedly dodgy credentials, she, along with Elizabeth I and Mary Queen of Scots, nevertheless completes an unofficial triumvirate of powerful and influential female rulers who dominated sixteenth-century Europe. Catherine's legacy as a sinister matriarch is such that she has even been a villain in a 1960s story of the classic sci-fi series *Doctor Who*.

Elisabeth of Valois – Henry II and Catherine de Medici's daughter and Mary's childhood playmate, and perhaps even her best friend of the France years, she was married off to Phillip II after his wife 'Bloody Mary', Elizabeth I's half-sister, died, dying herself in childbirth several years later.

Diane de Poiters – Henry II's glamorous older mistress, Diane had two daughters by her first marriage to Louis de Brézé. She wore black and white in mourning for him and continued to favour those colours for the rest of her life. Francis I, father of Henry II, assigned Diane to act as a mentor – and most likely far more than that – for his son. Diane held Henry in the palm of her hand until his death in the jousting accident of 1559, whereupon Catherine de Medici reclaimed all the jewels he had given her and effectively banished her from court. Nevertheless, during her time in the ascendancy Diane was as much responsible for the upbringing of the royal children at the French court – including Mary – as was Catherine herself; they even teamed up to boot out Mary Fleming's mother, Lady Fleming, after she became pregnant by Henry II and had the temerity to boast about her royal romp. One of Diane's most marvellous houses was Anet, near Dreux, west of Paris. The beautiful Diane was played by Hollywood legend Lana Turner in the 1956 movie *Diane*, which also starred 007 Roger Moore as Henry II.

Lady Fleming – Mary Fleming's mother, widowed after one of the many English incursions of the 'Rough Wooings', and who then had the good fortune to find herself in the French king's bed whilst acting in the role of Mary's governess; her boasting led to her quick expulsion from both court and country, courtesy of a rare truce between Catherine de Medici and Diane de Poiters.

Lady Parois – second, stricter French governess for Mary in the wake of the fall of Lady Fleming. Mary fell out with her over some old garments she donated and became convinced that Parois was poisoning her mother's mind against her in a series of letters that were sent to Mary of Guise.

Renee of Guise – Mary's aunt, and abbess of the Convent of Saint-Pierre at Rheims where Mary of Guise was buried and where Mary Seton retired after enduring seventeen years of captivity in England with her mistress.

Elizabeth I – briefly princess but rapidly bastardised daughter of Henry VIII and his second wife Anne Boleyn, Elizabeth was crowned Queen of England in 1558 after an upbringing fraught with danger and difficulty. She was a Protestant heroine to her nation but was also an upstart and a usurper to the rest of the still mainly Catholic world; the Pope went so far as to excommunicate her in 1570. Famous for being the 'virgin queen', she was nevertheless sexually savvy enough to be borderline neurotic about Mary's looks, position, and power, not to mention her fertility. She had her cousin kept in close captivity for nineteen years when Mary fled to her shores for help and flung herself on her mercy. Their twin legend has evolved cyclically throughout the generations, each woman in turn reinvented in one way or another for the appropriate audience. And yes, they never actually met, although the best fictional face-to-face is, in the author's opinion, Katharine Hepburn *v.* Florence Eldridge in the 1936 movie *Mary of Scotland*. Given her propensity for valuing style over substance, it would have been extremely galling for

Elizabeth I. (Wellcome Library, London)

Elizabeth to discover that in death Mary's tomb, just across the way from her own resting space at Westminster Abbey, was not only considerably costlier than her own, but also considerably grander to boot.

Lady Jean Stewart – also the Countess of Argyll, Jean was Mary's beloved half-sister, born several years earlier to James V and one of his many mistresses. She wins historical brownie points by being present in the supper room the night David Rizzio was murdered, preventing the whole thing being plunged into darkness by snatching up a candle as the supper table was overturned. Jean's marriage to the Earl of Argyll was famously unhappy and they finally divorced in 1573 after almost twenty years.

Margaret Carwood – one of Mary's maids-of-honour who may or may not have been among those who rode with her to Dunbar when she escaped from the scene of the Rizzio murder at Holyrood Palace.

Margaret Lennox – Darnley's mother and the daughter of Margaret Tudor by her second marriage to Archibald Douglas, she sought the ideal marriage for her son Darnley and got it, only to have him almost blown up and then decisively strangled for her pains. She became reconciled to Mary in later years, which is rather strong historical proof of the fact that Mary may have been innocent of any complicity in her husband's death; either that or she was as adept at spin as her accusers said she was.

Lady Jean Gordon – Bothwell's wife, whom he divorced in order to marry Mary. Strangely enough, especially given his robust reputation, she wasn't particularly bothered by the split, living until 1629 when she died at the exceedingly ripe old age of 83.

Lady Margaret Erskine – mother of Mary's illegitimate half-brother Moray, and resident of Lochleven Castle whilst Mary was imprisoned there. Mary's father James V nearly married Margaret Erskine but was unable to secure the papal dispensation necessary; she was married at the time and took his ultimate rejection of her rather badly. At the time of Mary's incarceration on Lochleven, Lady Erskine was wise enough to keep her options open and realise that, whilst she wanted her son Moray to be regent, she also was partial to the idea of one of her other sons, 'Pretty Geordie' Douglas, marrying the captive Scots queen with whom he seemed so taken.

Lady Scrope – sister of the Duke of Norfolk, she played matchmaker between her brother and the Queen of Scots whilst Mary was held at her husband's seat of Bolton Castle.

Jane Kennedy – one of Mary's ladies, Jane Kennedy actually possesses the coveted historical kudos of accompanying her mistress to the scaffold and even tying the white handkerchief around her eyes. She is recorded as having served the queen throughout the entirety of her captivity, which allows her to trump even the faithful Mary Seton for sheer staying power during the endless years of being ferried around various draughty English castles and stately homes. Unfortunately she endured all that only to be drowned two years after Mary's death, whilst assigned as part of the reception committee welcoming the prospective bride of James VI/I, Anne of Denmark, across to Scotland.

Maria Courcelles – another lady-in-waiting associated with the years of captivity, and one who may have departed from her mistress's service at the same time as Mary Seton.

Elizabeth Curll (or Curle) – sister of secretary Curll, Elizabeth also attended Mary at her execution along with Jane Kennedy, and went with Barbara Mowbray into exile; they were buried in St Andrew's church in Antwerp.

Barbara Mowbray – a latecomer to the years of Mary's captivity (1584), either she or Elizabeth Curll – or both – commissioned a portrait of Mary's execution during their later years in exile in Antwerp. Barbara was married to Mary's secretary Gilbert Curll, and bore him a child whilst at Chartley; Sir Amyas Paulet refused to allow a priest to baptise the child, so Mary stepped in and performed the ceremony herself. Rather unsurprisingly, both of Barbara's children became Jesuit priests.

Bess of Hardwick – Shrewsbury's second wife (he was her fourth husband) and an unusual example of a Tudor woman not only breaking through the glass ceiling, but then upending it and turning into a wall as well; 'Hardwick Hall, more glass than wall', so the rhyme says. She married in her teens the young heir Robert Barley, and then on his death took as her second husband Sir William Cavendish, with whom she had her many children. On his death she married Sir William St Loe, captain of the guard to Elizabeth I; on his death Bess gained all of his fortune and estates, much to the annoyance – putting it mildly – of his other children. Her fourth and last marriage was to George Talbot, the 6th Earl of Shrewsbury, one of the premier aristocrats of Elizabethan England, and marvellously minted to boot. Considering that she was now one of the richest women in the country, their combined fortunes served to make them almost England's premier power couple; they tied the knot in 1568. They enjoyed a few months of domestic bliss before Elizabeth I charged them with the custody of Mary Queen of Scots, a poisoned chalice if ever there was one. Bess was considered of sufficient 'quality' to sew with Mary, which she did on a regular basis, and their work is now on display at Oxburgh Hall and Holyrood Palace, among others. Bess must have gossiped a great deal during these Tudor/Stuart sewing bees because when the relationship between the Shrewsburys turned sour and Mary sent her infamous 'Scandal Letter' to Elizabeth, it was chock full of all the juiciest titbits to come from the Tudor court, and most of it highly defamatory to Elizabeth. The relationship between Bess and Mary had in fact started to sour when Bess married one of her daughters to Darnley's younger brother, hoping for a child of Tudor blood; she got this with the birth of Arbella Stuart and from that point on Mary became less of a talking point in her various households and instead more of a burden. Arbella, of course, had a claim to the throne, so Mary's own claim became something to be scuppered instead. Bess accused her husband of falling for Mary's legendary charms, and there may have been some truth in this; had Bess truly wanted to slander Mary she would perhaps have accused her of intimacy with a serving boy or someone of a scandalously lower social standing, so from her point of view perhaps Shrewsbury *was* overly attentive to Mary, but both of them had to tread a fine line with someone who might one day be their future queen. After Shrewsbury died in 1590 Bess went on building, including the aforementioned new version of Hardwick Hall. She didn't die herself until 1608, when all the main players in her little sewing bee drama were all long since departed for that rather bigger sewing bee in the sky.

Arbella Stuart – daughter of Charles Stuart, brother of Darnley, and one of Bess of Hardwick's daughters, Elisabeth Cavendish (from Bess's second marriage to Sir William Cavendish). Bess and Margaret Lennox risked everything to bring about the hasty union which would produce a viable heir to the throne of England. Poor Arbella was groomed for that throne and lived almost as miserable a life locked up in Hardwick Hall and various other residences as did Mary herself (who, as far as is known, was never actually locked up in Hardwick Hall). Long after Mary Queen of Scots was executed Arbella ended up in the Tower of London on the orders of James VI/I and starved herself to death.

Mary's Manors

The Scottish Sites

Linlithgow Palace – Mary's birthplace, located around 15 miles west of Edinburgh in the little town of Linlithgow. A castle or palace of some sort has existed on the site since the twelfth century, but the palace as it stands today has come down mainly from designs by James V and VI. A fire has left it a gutted but still rather impressive shell, and the fountain in the main courtyard is spectacular come rain or shine. The rooms where Mary was born are still visible, albeit the visitor needs to beware a crick in the neck when taking them in; the floor on which they were situated no longer exists and the best view is therefore from the still extant floor below. A statue of Mary is shortly to be erected in the grounds of Linlithgow Palace, having been championed by the Marie Stuart Society. Directly adjacent to the palace is St Michael's parish church, where Mary was baptised; there is a wood carving of her inside the church on one of the pulpits. The pub 'The Four Marys' is almost directly opposite Linlithgow Palace on the High Street, and sports a marvellous array of Mary memorabilia hanging from its walls, including countless portraits as well as copies of letters and newspaper articles. Mary's half-brother Moray was assassinated just down the road from the pub; turn left on leaving the pub and walk to the site of

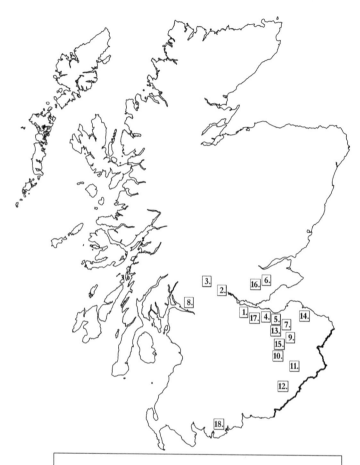

Mary's Scotland

1. Linlithgow Palace
2. Stirling Castle
3. Inchmahome Priory
4. Edinburgh Castle
5. Holyrood Palace
6. Falkland Palace
7. Craigmillar Castle
8. Dumbarton Castle
9. Critchton Castle

10. Traquair House
11. Jedburgh
12. Hermitage Castle
13. Kirk O'Field
14. Dunbar Castle
15. Borthwick Castle
16. Lochleven
17. Niddry Castle
18. Dundrennan Abbey

Mary's Scotland map.

the former Archbishop Hamilton's house, which is on the same side of the road; there is a plaque on the wall commemorating the fact.

Stirling Castle – set high above the town of Stirling, the castle is where Mary spent most of her early childhood and it remains virtually intact, although the chapel where she was baptised was razed to the ground. The 'Stirling Heads' are well worth a look, a collection of carved roundels depicting various kings, queens and courtiers, and the whole place was recently renovated for a more visitor-friendly feel; the sprawling golden great hall is, well, great. Views down into the town and the surrounding countryside are spectacular, again come rain or shine, and a walk down into said town will land you at the Darnley Coffee House on Bow Street. The Darnley Coffee House is situated on the site of a house the camp king was actually rumoured to have used as a bolthole when being blanked by English ambassadors all became a bit too much for him. Stirling Castle was also the site of Mary's son James' christening.

Inchmahome Priory – a small island on the Lake of Menteith close to Aberfoyle (north of Glasgow), where the young Mary was sent in order to save her from the marauding forces of the English during the 'Rough Wooings'; the peaceful, tranquil spot was the site of a settlement of Augustinian canons who had already been there for several hundred years when their little guest arrived. The place is now partially ruined, but it can be fun for the visitor to count how many places or spots are actually labelled as 'The Queen's ...' this or that. If forced to pick between them then the weary wanderer would be best put to plump for 'Queen Mary's Bower', the little circle of boxwood trees to the south-west of the cloister, although they were apparently replanted after Victorian visitors took so many cuttings as souvenirs that they literally stripped the original foliage almost down to nothing. Like many of the Scottish sites associated with Mary, Inchmahome is only open during the summer months.

Edinburgh Castle – famous for being the birthplace of Mary's son James, the castle sits at the top of the Royal Mile and can be seen for miles around, a bit like Stirling Castle in this respect. The small room where Mary gave birth still exists, as does the charming suite of chambers beyond. There is a small stump of a tree in the room where she gave birth which is supposed to have come from Lochleven. Edinburgh Castle was also where her mother, Mary of Guise, died and there is a plaque in the courtyard commemorating the fact; another plaque sits high up on the wall of the path into the castle just past the ticket office, commemorating Kirkcaldy of Grange, who held the castle for Mary's forces while she was in captivity, after having initially been an opponent of hers. He was beheaded for his troubles. Edinburgh Castle was also where Bothwell was imprisoned after allegedly plotting to kidnap Mary the first time around; it was said he escaped by scaling the sheer rock face with his bare hands before making his way down to the ground. Take a wander around the base of the castle at any angle and marvel at this manly feat of derring-do and then wonder if perhaps the tale that he was in fact simply let out of his cell by an ally might in fact be a little more likely.

Holyrood Palace – Mary's main Scottish residence and the scene of so many of her triumphs and tragedies, Holyrood Palace sits at almost the opposite end of the Royal Mile/Canongate to Edinburgh Castle. Her apartments in the west tower are largely unchanged from when she lived in them and the curious visitor can peer into the famous supper room, scene of the Rizzio tragedy, and even trace the trail of his corpse and stand in the exact spot where it was allegedly dumped in what was then her presence chamber (the red stain on the relatively recent wooden flooring is a shameless embellishment for the benefit of your average morbid tourist). That presence chamber, which lies adjacent to her bedchamber, is now full of portraits and relics including a lock of her hair and some of the tapestries she sewed with Bess of Hardwick; among these is the famous 'A Catte' piece showing a large, ginger tabby holding down a poor, maltreated mouse with its paw. Darnley's apartments –

Mary's Bath House, Holyrood. (BLFC, 001488127)

later used by Bothwell – are directly below Mary's, but the secret staircase between them has been bricked up; the outline of the doorway can be seen hidden behind a tapestry in Mary's bedroom itself, just on your left when entering from the main staircase from Darnley's apartments. The ceiling of Mary's bedroom, with the various heraldic carvings of the initials of her mother and father, are still marvellously intact as well. Holyrood Abbey, adjacent to the palace, is now ruinous, and the bones belonging to Darnley have long since been swiped by gruesome souvenir hunters, with his skull apparently ending up in the Royal College of Surgeons. The gardens of the palace are well worth a stroll if the weather is fine, but there are no remains whatsoever of any archery butts, or more excitingly the lion pit that Bothwell and Huntly allegedly vaulted whilst making their escape from the Rizzio murderers. On the edge of the road called Abbeyhill out at the front of Holyrood Palace (turn left if approaching from the Canongate, or right if leaving the palace) is a small stone building called 'Mary's Bath House'. This building was allegedly erected for Mary when she famously bathed in white wine; she may have used this on her face in order to preserve that perfect alabaster complexion, but whether she immersed her whole body in it is another matter. Most people bathed little more than three times a year, and Elizabeth I was considered strange because she bathed once a month!

Falkland Palace – located in Fife, Falkland Palace played host to the final hours of Mary's father James V, where he may or may not have uttered his famous line on the beginning and end of the Stuart dynasty. It also houses what is believed to be the oldest real tennis court in the world; Mary certainly played on it on several occasions. The palace, which in stylistic terms is heavily influenced by the French Renaissance, is largely intact and sits right in the centre of the town so it's very hard to miss. Mary visited occasionally, but despite the odd tennis game, Falkland Palace can't lay claim to being the scene of any of her more spectacular dramas, although it may have been here that she learned that Bothwell was perhaps planning to kidnap her the first time around.

Craigmillar Castle – several miles in the car or a bracing walk across or around Arthur's Seat away from Holyrood Palace, Craigmillar Castle is where the plot to do away with Darnley was originally hatched. Like Linlithgow it's a semi-ruined shell but a little less picturesque. Mary was said to have liked Craigmillar – some books cite it as being her favourite – but she was also extremely depressed here at around the time her marriage to Darnley really hit rock bottom, hence the plot and the signing of what has been termed 'The Craigmillar Bond' by various of her nobles. As with Linlithgow it's also well worth a visit, but like Linlithgow too many stone stairs can leave the joints a little sore. The area near to Craigmillar Castle is called 'Little France' because it was where many of Mary's French servants were quartered whenever she stayed there.

Dumbarton Castle – sitting upon a lump of volcanic rock, Dumbarton Castle, which overlooks the town of Dumbarton in West Dunbartonshire, was where the young Mary waved goodbye to her mother before she set sail for France as a young child in order to keep her from the clutches of the English. The castle is now mostly ruinous with just a few buildings extant, but this was one of the pivotal locations of the young Mary's life and the views from the top looking out onto the River Clyde are simply stunning. There are around five hundred steps in total, and some of the climbs are not for the faint-hearted. There is a plaque from the Marie Stuart Society commemorating the place the castle holds in Mary's history.

Crichton Castle – near the River Tyne in Midlothian, this former base of operations of Bothwell's was also the scene of the wedding of his sister to Mary's half-brother John Stewart, the lavish celebrations to which Mary attended in 1562. The castle is now – like Linlithgow and Craigmillar – a hollowed-out ruin but the walls inside the courtyard comprising an Italian influence are well worth a look. Bothwell's wife Jean Gordon kept Crichton when he divorced her in order to marry Mary, and it was said that he visited Jean there despite his new marriage, still considering her his wife and Mary merely his 'concubine', although this may well have been propaganda on the part of the rebel lords.

Traquair House – the oldest inhabited house in Scotland, lying somewhere between the borders and Edinburgh in the Tweeddale area; Mary and Darnley visited Traquair when their marital problems were about as pronounced as the syphilitic pustules shortly to break out on the would-be king's face. Mary apparently believed that she was pregnant whilst at Traquair and Darnley made some crass comment about Mary exerting herself on a hunt when she believed that she might be expecting again – the visit was shortly after the birth of baby James. This led the laird of Traquair to admonish Darnley for his discourteous conduct, which probably led to Darnley flouncing out with his tail between his legs. Again. Today Traquair is a tourist attraction boasting a bed Mary slept in – the genuine article, it appears, albeit actually used by her in a different location – as well as one of the cradles used for baby James VI/I.

Jedburgh – specifically Mary Queen of Scots House, where Mary stayed during the regular justice assizes held in the border areas, and where she suffered her subsequent bout of ill-health on returning from Bothwell's Hermitage; a 'near-death experience' might in fact be a better description. The house that the queen stayed in is now a free museum run partially on donations and dedicated wholly to Mary's memory. It houses countless works of art, relics and objects of interest, including the customary lock of hair and also a rather snazzy high-heeled shoe said to have been worn by Mary, as well as the watch she lost when falling from her horse whilst riding back from the Hermitage. Also of note is the gruesome photograph of Bothwell's mummified head, the real thing until recently on display in Dragsholm Castle in Denmark, and surely the only existing example of an actual photograph of one of the players in this fascinating period in history. One of the rooms houses a series of murals of all the major players in

Mary's story. On the High Street around the corner from Mary Queen of Scots House is the Spread Eagle Hotel, where Mary is also rumoured to have spent a night or two; the alleyway down the side is called 'Darnley's Close'.

Hermitage – Bothwell's formidable borders fortress, the imposing façade towers above the surrounding bleak borders countryside. It was here that an injured Bothwell was brought after a skirmish with 'Little Jock Elliot', which was later sung as a ballad called, imaginatively enough, 'Little Jock Elliot'. The Hermitage is where Mary rode to see the injured Bothwell whilst she was conducting justice assizes at nearby Jedburgh, completing the arduous round trip in a single day. Some have taken this feat to signify that Mary was traumatised by the wounding of her heroic hunk, but more likely she simply wanted to keep up the spirits of someone who was, if nothing else, fiercely loyal when compared to the rest of the backstabbers she was surrounded with. The elements have taken their toll on the building and the inside of the Hermitage is hollow but the façade is simply fantastic and worth the drive in order to see it; a car is almost essential to find this fabulous building, as is a heavy coat and some industrial strength hair product – the wind really

Hermitage Castle. (BLFC, 001859661)

whistles over those hillocks. The building and its surroundings are steeped in myth and legend, including the tale that anyone not born in the surrounding area will go mad if they spend a night within its walls. A woman in white wandering the grounds is believed to be the ghost of Mary, said to be searching out her 'beloved' Bothwell for one last tryst.

Kirk O'Field – the site of Darnley's murder, smack bang in the middle of Edinburgh, no longer exists; the site is now occupied by the University of Edinburgh. However, stand on the South Bridge Road directly in front of the university buildings and look right; the spot where Darnley's body was found, along with his valet, is said to be just in front of the Tesco's.

Dunbar Castle – located in the town of Dunbar in East Lothian, just a twenty-minute train ride from Edinburgh, this was the fortress that Mary fled to after the Rizzio murder; she then granted it to Bothwell and it was here that he allegedly abducted and raped her, holding her prisoner for ten days; or, if you believe the love stories of the likes of Jean Plaidy and Margaret George, not to mention the Katharine Hepburn movie, it's where they truly fell in love. More ruinous than most, it sits in the harbour on the edge of the North Sea and is in such a state of disrepair that it is now fenced off from the public and extreme caution is to be advised in approaching it. If the harbour bridge is down, you can get a different view of the castle by walking over and looking at it from that vantage point, but again caution is advised as a sudden gust of wind can cause even the hardiest of explorers to grab for the nearest available handhold. Dunbar Castle was pulled down after Bothwell fled from Scotland.

Borthwick Castle – a sturdy and wholly intact structure 12 miles south-east of Edinburgh, it was here that Mary and Bothwell fled after their wedding and where the fact that they essentially spent their 'honeymoon' is often traded on as one of the site's unique selling points. Mary is said to have abseiled down the back wall disguised as a boy when her rebel lords besieged them there, and visitors can stay in the room she and Bothwell shared because Borthwick Castle is now run as rather an expensive hotel. She also paraded back and forth across the battlements, trading insults with the rebel lords who had gathered in the courtyard below, and apparently gave as good as she got.

Lochleven – Mary spent almost eleven months here after being defeated by her rebel lords at the Battle of Carberry Hill. Like Inchmahome, Lochleven is located on an island, this time at Kinross, and as with Inchmahome, Historic Scotland also runs a boat service over to it several times a day. The castle is semi-ruinous and the island is rather small, but during Mary's stay it was apparently even smaller, with the water almost lapping up to the doors. The lake was drained several centuries later and it was then that the keys that Willie Douglas tossed into the water on her escape were said to have been found. The island has a rather melancholy feel to it, as it was here that Mary suffered a miscarriage, losing what were said to have been twins from her union – willing or otherwise – with Bothwell. On first arriving she also took to her bed and refused food or drink for a fortnight, so deep was her distress. She was also forced to abdicate here, under pain of being 'cut up into collops', which was a favourite threat of various of her backstabbing nobles; a 'collop' is a slice of meat. Because of the circumstances of her stay it lacks the romantic air of Inchmahome but still holds a pivotal place in her spectacular story.

Niddry Castle – Mary rested here after her extraordinary escape from Lochleven. Located in West Lothian it is now in private hands but can be viewed from a relatively discreet distance.

Dundrennan Abbey – Mary spent her last night on Scottish soil here before setting out on a small sailing boat for the coast of Cumberland – she landed in Workington – in what turned out to be perhaps the biggest mistake of her life. Today the abbey is semi-ruinous but still spectacular when viewed from several of the more flattering angles. A hearty walk of a mile or so from Dundrennan leads the explorer of Mary's many myths down to the banks of the Solway Firth and in particular the mouth of the Abbey Burnfoot (directions are best sought from the Dundrennan Abbey staff). A few sad remnants of the jetty survive, where the monks of this Cistercian monastery used to ship various wares out to Europe, and where Mary and her small retinue clambered onto their sailing boat before making their way to England.

The French Chateaus

Blois – located in the Loire Valley, Blois, like many of Mary's French residences, is still almost entirely intact. It sports one hundred rooms and the most striking feature to the visitor is the impressive outside spiral staircase. Blois is now a tourist attraction and open to the public.

Saint-Germain – whilst Oliver Cromwell busied himself by laying waste to many fine English and Scottish castles and houses during the Civil War, the French Revolution left almost all of the many marvellous palaces and houses that the young Mary Queen of Scots stayed in virtually intact. Such is the case with Saint-Germain, 19 kilometres west of Paris.

Fontainebleau – located some 55 kilometres outside of Paris, Fontainebleau remains one of the most spectacular of all the French chateaus that Mary spent time in whilst she was growing up in France. Today it is a school of the arts for American students.

Chambord – like Blois, Chambord is located in the Loire Valley, a great fairytale castle, lending its majesty to the idyllic romance of Mary's essentially carefree early years at the French court. Like Blois, it is also now a major tourist attraction and open to the public. Among those allegedly responsible for its design is Da Vinci himself.

Mary's France

1. Roscoff
2. Saint-Germain
3. Fontainebleau
4. Chambord
5. Anet
6. Amboise
7. Notre Dame
8. Rheims
9. Blois
10. Calais

Mary's France map.

Anet – built for Diane de Poiters, Anet is located near Dreux in France, and was one of the favourite retreats of the French children when Mary was growing up with them during her time in France. Anet has been partially demolished but the house that stands today is still in part composed of the original building. Anet was used as a location for the James Bond film *Thunderball* in 1965 and also *The Pink Panther Strikes Again* in 1976.

Amboise – notorious, as far as Mary Queen of Scots is concerned, for being the site of the massacre of the rebels who attempted to overthrow the rule of the Guises in 1560. It seems inconceivable that Mary, who was apt to faint at the sight of one botched execution, was witness to the slaughter that went on here. By the time it was done the smell of death was so bad that the court had to leave. Amboise sits serenely in front of the River Loire, and Leonardo da Vinci is buried in the nearby chapel of Saint-Hubert.

The English Prisons

Carlisle Castle – the first of Mary's many English prisons, where she was kept for almost two months in the care of Sir Francis Knollys from May 1568; Mary Seton was one among many of her loyal supporters who joined her here after making the journey from Scotland under their own volition. Mary is said to have observed a game of football played in the grounds between her supporters and the castle's garrison. She also worshipped at the cathedral nearby. Carlisle Castle is still a vast and sprawling structure despite having undergone several changes down the centuries. The tower in which Mary resided in the south-east corner has been demolished but the main castle structure is sound and impressive, with views to the mountains of Scotland visible from the battlements.

Bolton Castle – located in remote Wensleydale in North Yorkshire, the castle is located at a beautiful but relatively remote spot, visitors to which will probably require a car. Mary spent six months here,

Mary's England

1. Workington Hall
2. Cockermouth
3. Carlisle Castle
4. Bolton Castle
5. Tutbury Castle
6. Wingfield Manor
7. Chatsworth
8. St Mary's Guildhall, Coventry

9. Sheffield Castle & Manor Lodge
10. Old Hall, Buxton
11. Worksop Manor
12. Chartley Manor
13. Tixall Manor
14. Fotheringay Castle
15. Peterborough Cathedral
16. Westminster Abbey

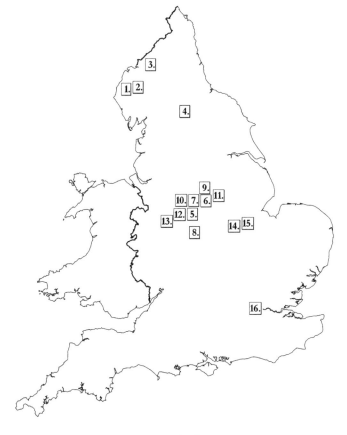

Mary's England map.

hot on the heels of Carlisle, again in the care of Sir Francis Knollys and also of Lord Scrope, who actually owned the place. The shell of this impressive fortress is intact and the inside has some visitor attractions but parts are crumbling; the views however, especially on a sunny day, are simply breathtaking. Mary was here when the inquiry into the matter of her guilt over Darnley's death, which introduced to the world the controversy of the Casket Letters, was being held in York. 'The Queen's Gap', the point at which Mary is said to have reached during an escape attempt, is nearby.

Tutbury Castle – the first of the Shrewsbury properties to which Mary was brought when she passed into their custody, Tutbury Castle sits on a hill in the middle of the village of the same name, in rural Staffordshire. It was here that Mary was introduced to her custodians for the next fourteen years, George Talbot, 6th Earl of Shrewsbury and his wife, Bess of Hardwick. Mary hated Tutbury because of its position on said hill, where it was 'exposed to all the winds and inclemencies of Heaven'. Her rooms were located near the toilets or 'privies' which were emptied out only once a week, usually on a Saturday morning; this makes for a good sound bite but may only have been the case when Paulet was her jailer and the terms of her incarceration much harsher. The Shrewsburys used Tutbury mainly as a hunting lodge and didn't care much for it either, arranging a removal to nearby Wingfield Manor as soon as was possible. Today Tutbury is a top tourist attraction, with countless events held during the summer for all the family. It is semi-ruinous. It was also the location for an episode of *Most Haunted*, during which 'psychic' Derek Acorah was apparently accosted by the ghost of Paulet.

Wingfield Manor – located in Alfreton in Derbyshire, Wingfield Manor is a stunning shell of a manor house, looming out of the surrounding countryside on the top of a relatively steep hill surrounded by woodland and several private fishing lakes. Mary stayed here after her initial sojourn at Tutbury and enjoyed greater freedom and certainly even greater views; English Heritage take tours around the site several times a year but it is best to book in advance.

At other times it is a private working farm and due courtesy should be paid to the owner. Mary returned to Wingfield again after leaving the custody of the Earl of Shrewsbury, when Sir Ralph Sadler was temporarily tasked with the thankless position. Like Tutbury Castle it is semi-ruinous. The old walnut tree said to have come from a seed dropped by Anthony Babington is unfortunately just one of the many myths that circulate around the Scots queen, as it is growing in what would at that time have been an indoor part of the building.

Chatsworth – standing on the east bank of the River Derwent in Derbyshire, Chatsworth was one of the more picturesque of Mary's many prisons. The original turreted house built by Bess of Hardwick has long since vanished but the current Chatsworth House is built on the site of the original in which Mary stayed. A suite of rooms in the new house have been named after her and are said to occupy the same space as those in the original. The small, moated structure in the grounds called 'Mary's Bower' may have been used by Mary to take her exercise; the Hunting Tower at the back of the house, reached by a steep walk through dense forest, definitely dates from the period of her stay. Cecil visited Mary at Chatsworth to discuss terms for her release and it was here that the Rollestons and several others plotted to free her and spirit her away over the hills. Those rolling hills surrounding Chatsworth are simply stunning, and also recommended is the nearby little village of Edensor, a quick walk away; one of Mary's servants, John Beaton, was interred in the church there and the brass plaque to him remains on the left side of the chancel.

Sheffield Castle – this mighty structure, seated at the confluence between the River Sheaf and the River Don in Sheffield city centre, was Mary's main residence during her years as a 'guest' of the Shrewsburys. Unfortunately it was razed to the ground during the English Civil War and now almost nothing remains to be seen. However, excavations have begun and the market – aptly called 'Castle Market' – built over the site has been cleared so that major archaeological work can be undertaken. A group called the Friends of Sheffield Castle have been instrumental in promoting this work. Sheffield Castle may have been Shrewsbury's main residence but Mary is said to have loathed it, although this may have been due more to the longevity of her stay there than for any other reason; it is hard to imagine one of the premier noblemen in the country having as his main residence a dwelling that was anything less than stately, at the very least. Mary was housed at Sheffield Castle during the Ridolfi Plot and was apparently kept to her rooms for a staggering ten weeks at the height of the subsequent security scare. At other times she was allowed to walk on the leads (battlements) of the castle and in the courtyard, and on one particularly touching occasion Shrewsbury took her out for a brief constitutional during a deep snowfall, knowing that the risk of an escape at such a time was negligible; Mary is said to have leapt at the chance of a little fresh air. On another occasion a minor earthquake broke up the monotony of her stay!

Sheffield Manor Lodge – built as an alternative to Sheffield Castle and used mainly as a quick way of accommodating Mary and her retinue when the main fortress needed 'sweetening', what now remains of Sheffield Manor Lodge sits at the top of Sheffield and smack bang in the middle of the Manor Lane housing estate. When Mary was

Sheffield Manor Lodge. (BLFC, 003589731)

shuttled between the two residences, the path that separated the two was said to have been lined with oaks, giving on to a large park. The turret house, which may have been built specifically for Mary to take the air and from which she might watch the hunt, is entirely intact and perhaps the best preserved example of one of her English prisons; the ornamental ceilings inside have been restored and are well worth a look. The Friends of Sheffield Manor Lodge help run the site as a tourist attraction with a specially designed visitor centre, giving costumed talks and open days for the whole family.

Buxton Old Hall – now reputedly the oldest hotel in the country, Buxton Old Hall was built as a townhouse for Mary and her entourage to use whilst taking the famous restorative waters which made Buxton famous. It is debatable which part of the current Buxton Old Hall Hotel is actually comprised of the original structure, but the management seem confident enough to have called the largest suite 'Mary's Bower', and besides this the place is a veritable marvel of Mary portraiture and merchandise. Adjacent to the Old Hall is an actual spring, St Ann's Well, the water from which is drinkable. One of the many legends that surround Mary says that she gave alms to a beggar standing right by the well, and was strictly admonished by Shrewsbury as a result. Certain enough was the fact that the town was all but closed off to visitors when Mary was in residence, but she may have met both her old and unwilling suitor the Earl of Leicester there, as well as Cecil.

Whilst at Buxton Mary may also have visited Poole's Cavern, a nearby natural limestone cave, and one of the stalactites is named after her. It is not inconceivable that the sometimes lenient Shrewsbury may have organised such a trip, especially in light of the fact that he wasn't averse to letting his captive have a little caper in the snow, but how much a woman afflicted by rheumatism brought about by years of captivity could have negotiated such a treacherous underground path is open to speculation. It is possible, however, that Mary might have visited Poole's Cavern during her first visit to Buxton when she had only been a captive for a couple of years and was still relatively mobile.

Worksop Manor – Shrewsbury began building Worksop Manor whilst Mary was in his custody, which rather gives the lie to his frequent pleas of poverty; Mary stayed here twice toward the end of her time with the Shrewsburys, when their much publicised marital problems were reaching their peak. Shrewsbury was reprimanded for allegedly allowing Mary to take a walk through the nearby Sherwood Forest, although he strongly denied it. The original structure burnt down and the house on the present site is a private stud farm, with the emphasis on *private*.

St Mary's Guildhall, Coventry – Mary was moved to Coventry as a matter of some urgency to keep her out of the clutches of Northumberland and Westmorland during the 'Rising of the North'. Initially Mary was lodged at the nearby Bull Inn (long since lost) but Elizabeth thought that not a fit place for a queen and she was moved to the Guildhall, where the rooms she is said to have stayed in can be viewed by the public. Visitors may choose either the poky little set of rooms on the third floor – Caesar's Tower – or more likely the Mayoress's Parlour as the site of her actual stay. She was moved to several other residences around Coventry during her stay but records are sketchy and the only other possible location for her is the nearby Whitefriars Monastery.

Chartley Manor – Mary was moved here after a stint at Tutbury under the watch of her strict new jailer Sir Amyas Paulet. The moated house belonged to Elizabeth's young favourite and

Chartley Manor. (Staffordshire Museum Service)

sometime Tudor toy boy the Earl of Essex, and it was here that the Babington Plot took place, with Mary receiving her secret – and monitored – correspondence from Anthony Babington in barrels of beer brought from a brewer in Burton. That brewer was nicknamed 'The Honest Man' because he was taking payment from Mary as well as from Paulet. Today, Chartley Manor is a very private residence and all but invisible from the busy A518. The *Elizabeth R* episode entitled 'Horrible Conspiracies', which starred Vivian Pickles as Mary, is set at Chartley. Despite what many books may say, Mary never stayed at Chartley Castle, the ruins of which are in the field adjacent to the moated house, and which are, however, slightly more visible from the busy A518.

Tixall Hall – Mary was taken to Tixall Hall, home of the Aston family, after her part in the Babington Plot was uncovered. She was arrested somewhere in Tixall Park, dismounting from her horse and sitting on the ground, from where she refused to move; the exact spot is unknown. Today all that remains of Tixall Hall is the impressive gatehouse, which is now available for private rent. It was through here that Mary passed on her way back to her ransacked rooms at Chartley, telling the waiting beggars that she had nothing to give them because she was now as poor and destitute as they themselves were.

Tixall Gatehouse. (BLFC, 000725989)

Fotheringay Castle – the site of Mary's final prison and also that of her execution is, like her main residence of Sheffield Castle, now almost utterly erased from the landscape. Located in the charming little village of Fotheringay, the site of the castle is now a scheduled monument. It was a large motte and bailey castle, and the hill upon which the keep itself stood is still littered with little pieces of rubble, most of them protruding through the grass; visitors may walk the length of the now dry moat around it.

One single chunk of masonry remains from the castle and is carefully preserved close by, with a plaque; visitors and pilgrims leave flowers and pictures of Mary here. The Scottish thistles – 'Queen Mary's Tears' – which sprout up all over the hill are said to have materialised there as a memorial to the Queen of Scots. Mary stood trial here and was executed on 8 February 1587. James VI/I didn't have the castle demolished because of the slight to his mother's memory, as popular legend declares; instead it simply fell to ruin and was finally demolished some fifty years after her death. The Talbot Hotel in nearby Oundle is built from stones from the castle and several of the windows are also from Fotheringay, although the pedigree of the staircase, said to be the one down

Remains of Fotheringay Castle. (BLFC, 000247776)

The staircase at the Talbot Hotel, Oundle.
(BLFC, 000247776)

which Mary descended to her doom, is slightly more dubious. There is a mark in the wood said to have been made by Mary pressing her ring into it as she passed, but considering she was crippled with rheumatism and had to be supported by two guards this is extremely unlikely; even a healthy woman would have needed to channel superhuman strength to secure such an indentation.

8

Mary at the Movies

Mary of Scotland (1936) starring Katharine Hepburn as Mary – the 1936 RKO movie was the first big screen outing for Mary, with Katharine Hepburn cast as the Scots queen and Frederic March as a Bothwell most definitely more in the mould of romantic hero. Although it was something of a flop at the time, it is now considered by critics as a semi-classic. Moroni Olsen plays probably the most visually accurate John Knox ever seen on screen; little wonder as he had previously played him on the stage and thus was specially picked for the part here. Hepburn plays Mary as a somewhat tremulous tragic queen, who seems to spend the nineteen years of her English captivity in one solitary room! Florence Eldridge is an underrated Elizabeth I and their brief, fiery exchange at the end of the movie must be worth the price of the DVD alone. The musical numbers – mainly bagpipes played by Bothwell's band of brigands – make this movie at times a little like a black and white period version of *The Wizard of Oz*, especially in the scene where the populace of Edinburgh serenade a joyous Mary at her window, only to have John Knox literally materialise in their midst like 'The Wicked Witch of the West'. Joan Crawford played Mary in a later radio version (1937).

Das Herz der Konigin (*The Heart of the Queen*) (1940) starring Swedish chanteuse Zarah Leander as Mary – also Willy Birgel as Bothwell. This German movie, made during the Second World War, took Mary's story and made it a tool of Nazi propaganda;

the production was decidedly anti-British, with an Elizabeth – Maria Koppenhofer – even more cold, calculating, and intent on empire building than usual. It's worth watching for the fact of its highly unusual social significance, but Birgel makes for a slimy Bothwell, and Leander – who breaks into song several times during the movie – is somewhat cold and distant herself as Mary.

Sir Francis Drake (TV series; 1961) with Noelle Middleton as Mary – the episode entitled 'Queen of Scots' is set at Tutbury Castle during the time she was held there under the watch of Sir Amyas Paulet, around late 1585; moody, atmospheric black and white drama or pure teatime kids' kitsch adventure yarn, depending on your point of view. Jean Kent does a fine turn as a decidedly sympathetic Elizabeth I; Kent played Elizabeth throughout the series, appearing in all but a few of the episodes.

The Queen's Traitor (TV series; 1967) with Stephanie Beacham as Mary – all five episodes of this drama starring 'Dynasty' and 'Bad Girls' actress Stephanie Beacham are now lost from the archives, but it took place during the Ridolfi Plot when Mary was a captive at Sheffield Castle, and it involved her relationship with the Duke of Norfolk, after whom one assumes the entire thing was named.

Elizabeth R (TV series; 1971) with Vivian Pickles as Mary – Mary cameos in episode two, 'The Marriage Game', and is the focus of episode four, 'Horrible Conspiracies', set during the Babington Plot, when she was a resident at Chartley Manor; Hamilton Dyce plays a suitably sadistic Paulet, and Glenda Jackson won an Emmy for her role as Elizabeth. The whole thing may come across as somewhat stagey to a modern audience but it can't be faulted in terms of historical accuracy, and everyone is giving it their all. It also features Richard Topcliffe, Elizabeth's famously sadistic priest hunter, in what may be his only onscreen outing, played here by the slightly less sinister Brian Wilde ('Foggy' from *Last of the Summer Wine*).

Mary Queen of Scots (1971) starring Vanessa Redgrave as Mary – Glenda Jackson reprised her role as Elizabeth I from *Elizabeth R* to star alongside Vanessa Redgrave in this epic historical drama; the meeting of the two queens isn't quite as well done as it was in *Mary of Scotland*, and Nigel Davenport is a less dishy Bothwell, but it's still a good, solid historical epic. Some of the locations were authentic, if chronologically inaccurate; Bothwell's Hermitage was used as one of the locations, albeit as the place where Mary gave birth to her son. Mercifully Mary manages to see out the nineteen years of her captivity in more than just one room. The film received several Golden Globe nominations and does a good job of pointing out how much of a backstabber Mary's half-brother Moray was, if nothing else.

A Traveller in Time (TV series; 1978) with Heather Chasen as Mary – adapted from the Alison Uttley book of the same name, the story is set around the Babington home of Dethick Manor Farm, and concerns Anthony Babington's plans to free Mary from nearby Wingfield Manor, whilst at the same time trying to contest with a girl working in his house who has apparently travelled back in time because of her affinity to the tragic queen; the episodes have yet to be released officially by the BBC.

Gunpowder, Treason and Plot (TV series; 2004) with Clemence Poesy as Mary – a two-part gritty take on the plot that befell Darnley and the one that almost befell his father some thirty-odd years later. Clemence Poesy makes for a rather gobby, moody and modern Mary but there are nice little touches of authenticity, and her relationship with Kevin McKidd's Bothwell has a nice touch of plausibility to it. The second half, concentrating on her son James VI/I, is worth seeing simply because there aren't that many dramas or films about him and also because Robert Carlyle manages to make him likeable despite his many character defects. Michael Fassbender of *X-Men* fame makes for a good Guy Fawkes.

Elizabeth I (TV series; 2005) with Barbara Flynn as Mary – Mary is shown here in the later stages of her captivity and with yet another imagined meeting with Elizabeth; her execution is played out in graphic detail, right down to the botched job Bull the executioner made of it. Barbara Flynn plays Mary with a French accent, something that has always divided opinion, given that reports of Mary – at least at the time she was in captivity in England and specifically when observed at Tutbury Castle – said that she spoke with 'a pretty Scottish accent'. Helen Mirren makes for a fine Elizabeth but supporters of Mary might be a little less enchanted with the programme's rather rancid portrayal of her Scots cousin.

The Virgin Queen (TV series; 2005) with Charlotte Winner as Mary – not much Mary to be had here, just a rather underwhelming cameo from Charlotte Winner; Anne-Marie Duff is far more watchable as a decidedly earthy Elizabeth I, and the soundtrack is simply superb.

Elizabeth – The Golden Age (2007) with Samantha Morton as Mary – she might look a little young for Fotheringay but Samantha Morton might be the best of the onscreen Marys; she has the 'pretty Scottish accent' and the soft, curling auburn hair to a tee, plus a great line in Elizabeth I put-downs. The execution scene is marvellously recreated and Cate Blanchett is great at showing that Elizabeth didn't actually want to do it. Eilean Donan Castle in Scotland stands in for Fotheringay, and the Babington plotters put in an appearance, courtesy of actors Rhys Ifans and Eddie Redmayne, with Tom Hollander as Paulet.

Mary Queen of Scots (2013) with Camille Rutherford as Mary – another French-sounding Mary, this one did very well at the Toronto International Film Festival, and had a prestigious premiere in Glasgow, but as of this writing it hasn't yet seen general release in the UK.

Reign (TV series; 2013–present) with Adelaide Kane as Mary – a teen drama made in the US and following Mary's life at the French court; this series needs to be taken with a far larger dose of scepticism than its unofficial predecessor *The Tudors*, which got a lot more right than most people give it credit for. Here, just for starters, the famous Four Maries are replaced by four girl band wannabes called Kenna, Aylee, Lola, and Greer. A second season has been given the green light, but whether it will follow historical fact – unlikely – and take Mary back to Scotland remains to be seen. Megan Follows plays Catherine de Medici, and Alan van Sprang of *The Tudors* is King Henry II.

Mary Queen of Scots (2014) with Saoirse Ronan as Mary – currently or at least rumoured to be in production.

... and at the Theatre

Schiller's *Mary Stuart* – this play was originally performed in 1800 although it has been put on show by many different companies many times since. The play concerns Mary's final days and is broken up into five acts. It again shows a fictional meeting between the two queens, and Mary is once more brought down by the badly orchestrated Babington Plot, this time aided by a fictitious nephew of one of her custodians called 'Mortimer'. The play was the inspiration for...

Donizetti's *Mary Stuart* opera (based on the play) – by Gaetano Donizetti, this was first performed in 1834 and like the play *Mary Stuart* has of course been in production many times since. The differences between the play and the opera are various, Mary sometimes residing at Chatsworth where she and Elizabeth meet in the sprawling grounds, whilst at other times Mary has already reached her final destination of Fotheringay. Perhaps one of the most popular modern plays about Mary is *Mary Queen of Scots got her head chopped off* (1987), by the Scottish poet Liz Lochhead.

... and in Fiction

Mary has been the tragic, romantic heroine in fiction for so many
writers that a list of the complete works could fill a library all by
itself. The tales have been told from generation to generation so
that they evolve cyclically, with the current trends and sensibilities
being woven throughout the traditional narrative fabric of her life.
The real cult of the tragic queen was taken up by the Victorians, who
had a virtual mania for all things Mary. Reportedly a young child
once asked Queen Victoria if she was descended from Elizabeth I
and the queen indignantly replied that not a drop of her blood was
descended from that cruel tyrant, but that she could proudly point to
her heritage as having come from the kindly Queen of Scots. Among
the more modern novels about Mary are those written by Jean
Plaidy – *Royal Road to Fotheringay* – and its sequel, *The Captive
Queen of Scots*; also Margaret George's massive *Mary Queen of
Scotland and the Isles*; Alison Uttley's *A Traveller in Time*, about a
young girl from the present who finds herself suddenly transported
back to the Derbyshire home of Anthony Babington as he prepares
to rescue Mary from Wingfield Manor; Philippa Gregory's
The Other Queen, which details Mary's early years in the custody of
the Shrewsburys and the possible love felt for her by George Talbot;
and Reay Tannahill's marvellous *Fatal Majesty*, telling the tale of
Mary's time in Scotland mainly from Maitland's point of view.

Other characters involved with Mary have also appeared in the
pages of fiction. Bothwell has been brought to life in Margaret
Irwin's *The Galliard*, as well as more recently in *Lord James* by
Catherine Hermary-Vieille. Anthony Babington is the star of Jane
Lane's *Conies in the Hay*. There are several novels showcasing Bess
of Hardwick, among them Virginia Henley's *A Woman of Passion*;
even peripheral characters such as Patrick, Master of Gray get in
on the act, starring in his very own trilogy by Nigel Tranter. Where
Elizabeth I herself is concerned there are of course countless novels,
and far too many to mention here; undoubtedly because of their
interlinking myth Mary will get at least a namecheck in most of them.

Mary Merchandise

Mary is, as perhaps the most famous woman in Scotland, a highly marketable asset in the consumer-driven 21st century. As well as the books and the films there are Mary dolls, maquettes, playing cards, pill boxes, cushions and pillows, postcards, cutlery, coasters, and countless other related items; just search any online auction site and you will soon have a fair idea of what a magnet she is in terms of merchandising. You can download Mary Queen of Scots apps for your smartphone, as well as purchasing collectible cigarette cards, mouse mats, and countless other items. There are even do-it-yourself replicas of some of the embroidery Mary sewed whilst she was in captivity, including the famous 'A Catte'. You can also buy replica coins, pens and pencils, mugs and tablet covers.

Mary's Memory

Today Mary Queen of Scots is something of a national heroine in Scotland, and as such they market her image to within an inch of its life. There were several calls for her to be canonised by the Vatican as a Catholic saint in the nineteenth century, but thus far they have been refused on the grounds that it is as yet impossible to determine the extent – if any – of her involvement in her husband's murder. The secret archives of the Vatican state that the file on her canonisation is 'still open'. Mary's tomb at Westminster Abbey is visited by countless tourists, and some speak of the site as being a place of 'miracles'.

Whilst she was in captivity Mary made her own motto that had previously belonged to her mother, Mary of Guise. It was 'In my end is my beginning' (the French translation is *En ma fin est mon commencement*). She had it embroidered onto her cloth of state and when it was observed by a visitor to her at Tutbury Castle, one Nicholas White, he wrote to William Cecil saying that he had seen the motto but that he did not understand what it meant. Only now, hundreds of years later, does the meaning really become clear: in Mary's end, with her execution, so began her unending life as a living legend. It was almost as though she had dreamt of her own destiny as the great romantic, tragic queen of film and fiction, and whilst the dream soon left her, the memory of some great destiny was perhaps marked so indelibly on her mind that she sought to secure it somehow. How fitting for her that the dream turned out to be true.

A Queen's Chronology

1542

Nov	Battle of Solway Moss
8 Dec	Mary born
14 Dec	James V dies, battle weary

1543

1 July	Treaty of Greenwich, infant Mary to wed Henry VIII's son Edward VI
9 Sept	Mary crowned Queen of Scots

1544

	Henry VIII begins 'Rough Wooing' of Scotland to force the marriage of Mary and Edward

1547

28 Jan	Death of Henry VIII
20 Feb	Edward VI becomes King of England
10 Sept	Battle of Pinkie; Scots resolve to send Mary to France

1548

July	Mary sails for France
13 Aug	Mary arrives in France

1558

19 Apr	Mary betrothed to the Dauphin
24 Apr	Mary marries the Dauphin
17 Nov	Elizabeth I becomes Queen of England

1559

10 July	Henry II of France dies; Mary becomes Queen of France, with Francis as Francis II

1560

11 June	Mary of Guise dies in Scotland
10 July	Scottish Reformation Parliament; Protestant Kirk created
5 Dec	the Dauphin, now Francis II of France, dies; Mary widowed

1561

19 Aug	Mary arrives back in Scotland to take up the reins of power

1562

Sept	Mary's half-brother becomes Earl of Moray

1563

Feb	Chastelard 'stalker' incident
18 Feb	Duke of Guise, her uncle, assassinated in France

1564

March	Elizabeth I urges Mary to marry Robert Dudley

1565

17 Feb	Mary meets Darnley at Wemyss Castle
29 July	Mary marries Darnley
Aug–Sept	'Chaseabout Raid'

1566

9 March	David Rizzio murdered in Holyrood

19 June	Mary gives birth to James VI/I at Edinburgh Castle
15/16 Oct	Mary rides to Bothwell at the Hermitage, and falls ill on returning to Jedburgh
17 Dec	James baptised at Stirling
24 Dec	Mary pardons Rizzio plotters

1567

Jan	Darnley in Glasgow with syphilis
20/21 Jan	Mary visits and brings him back
10 Feb	Darnley assassinated at Kirk O'Field in Edinburgh
12 Apr	Bothwell acquitted of the murder
19/20 Apr	Ainslie's Tavern bond
24 Apr	Mary abducted by Bothwell to Dunbar
15 May	Mary marries Bothwell at Holyrood
15 June	Battle of Carberry Hill; Mary surrenders and Bothwell flees
17 June	Mary imprisoned on Lochleven
24 July	Mary forced to abdicate
29 July	Baby James crowned king at Stirling
22 Aug	Moray proclaimed regent

1568

Jan	Bothwell captured in Denmark
2 May	Mary escapes from Lochleven
13 May	Battle of Langside, Mary flees south
16 May	Mary crosses Solway Firth into England
18 May	Mary at Carlisle Castle
13 July	Mary taken to Bolton Castle in Wensleydale
Oct–Dec	Commission held in York to examine her guilt; Moray produces Casket Letters as evidence

1569

| Jan | Mary neither found guilty nor exonerated; Moray leaves to resume regency in Scotland, leaving his half-sister a political prisoner in England |

26 Jan	Mary sets out for Tutbury, to be handed into the custodianship of the Earl of Shrewsbury and his wife, Bess of Hardwick
20 Apr	Mary transferred to Wingfield Manor
21 Sept	Return to Tutbury
25 Nov	Northern Rebellion; Mary taken to Coventry to keep her from the liberating Northern Earls

1570

2 Jan	Back at Tutbury
23 Jan	Moray assassinated at Linlithgow
27 Apr	Papal bull excommunicates Elizabeth I
24/25 May	Mary transferred to Chatsworth
Oct	Visited at Chatsworth by Cecil
28 Nov	Transferred to Shrewsbury's main home of Sheffield Castle, her main prison for the next fourteen years

1571

4 Sept	Lennox killed
Sept	Ridolfi Plot
Nov–Dec	Cecil publishes knowledge of Mary's involvement in Darnley murder

1572

2 June	Duke of Norfolk executed for involvement in Ridolfi Plot
Aug	Massacre of St Bartholomew's Eve in France
24 Nov	Morton becomes regent

1573

25 Apr	Mary taken to Sheffield Manor Lodge
June	Bothwell taken to Dragsholm Castle
21/22 Aug	Mary's first visit to Buxton, to take the waters

1574

| 22 Feb | Henry III becomes King of France |

1578

14 Apr	Bothwell dies at Dragsholm
	Personal rule of James VI/I begins in Scotland

1581

2 June	Morton executed for role in Darnley's murder

1583

Nov	Throckmorton Plot

1584

Aug	Mary leaves Shrewsbury's custody, transferred to Sir Ralph Sadler's 'care'
Oct	Bond of Association enacted by English government

1585

4 Jan	Sir Amyas Paulet named as next custodian
14 Jan	Mary returns to Tutbury with Sir Ralph Sadler
Apr	Paulet arrives at Tutbury to take custodianship
24 Dec	Mary moved to Chartley Manor

1586

17 July	Mary writes to Anthony Babington
11 Aug	Mary arrested and taken to Tixall Hall
25 Sept	Mary taken to Fotheringay
14/15 Oct	Mary 'on trial' at Fotheringay
25 Oct	Commission in London finds Mary guilty
Nov	Sir Drue Drury arrives to assist Paulet

1587

1 Feb	Elizabeth signs Mary's death warrant
3 Feb	Privy Council despatch warrant without her knowledge
7 Feb	Mary told of execution
8 Feb	Mary executed

Afterword

Mickey Mayhew's book has provided you with the almost unbelievable story of the most romantic and enigmatic queen in the history of Scotland. It is a story which begins with adventure and almost fairy-tale events of the life of a little girl, spirited away from a warring cold country into the warmth and riches of a civilised court in Europe, to the romance of a childhood love and marriage and the unexpected early crowning of a young woman to become queen of two nations.

Because of jealousy and conniving at the French court it became necessary for this young widowed queen to return to her own native land and seat of her undisputed sovereignty. Facing a country whose people were unaccustomed to the rule of a woman and whose loyalty lay with their clan chiefs, life was a bewildering and complete contrast to this young woman who was a spoilt beauty at the renaissance and Roman Catholic court of France.

Judging her today, we would say that she was truly European in her outlook, and her tolerance to the newly Protestant religion of Scotland was in keeping with the twenty-first century attitude, not only to religion but to all ethical tastes and contrasts.

She fought hard to be accepted as an educated woman in a man's world – but living in an unenlightened sixteenth-century Scotland, she lost this battle.

From a distance of nearly 500 years, we can only admire her courage, determination, tolerance, kindness and patience in accepting nearly twenty years of confinement and insult.

With extensive study we can continue to seek to find the real Mary Queen of Scots, the real woman at the heart of a disturbed period in the history of Scotland, and who is the progenitor of the current royal family in Great Britain today.

Margaret C. Lumsdaine
President of the Marie Stuart Society
2015

Mary's Heraldic Arms. (Marie Stuart Society)

Bibliography and Further Reading

Bingham, Caroline, *Darnley* (London: Constable, 1995)

Bingham, Madeleine, *Scotland under Mary Stuart* (London: Book Club Associates, 1974)

Cheetham, J. Keith, *On the Trail of Mary Queen of Scots* (Edinburgh: Luath Press Ltd, 1999)

Dobson, Michael & Watson, Nicola J., *England's Elizabeth* (Oxford: Oxford University Press, 2002)

Doran, Susan, *Mary Queen of Scots – An Illustrated Life* (London: The British Library, 2007)

Edwards, Francis, *The Dangerous Queen* (London: Geoffrey Chapman, 1964)

Fraser, Antonia, *Mary Queen of Scots* (London: Phoenix, 2009, 40th anniversary edition)

George, Margaret, *Mary Queen of Scotland and the Isles* (London: Pan Books, 1992)

Gore-Browne, Robert, *Lord Bothwell* (London: Collins, 1937)

Graham, Roderick, *An Accidental Tragedy – The Life of Mary Queen of Scots* (Edinburgh: Birlinn, 2009)

Gregory, Philippa, *The Other Queen* (London: Harper, 2011)

Guy, John, *My Heart is My Own – The Life of Mary Queen of Scots* (London: Fourth Estate, 2009)

Leader, John Daniel, *Mary Queen of Scots in Captivity* (Sheffield: Leader & Sons, 1880)

Lewis, Jayne Elizabeth, *Mary Queen of Scots – Romance and Nation* (London: Routledge, 1998)

Mackay, James, *In My End is My Beginning – A Life of Mary Queen of Scots* (Edinburgh: Mainstream Publishing, 1999)

Plaidy, Jean, *Mary Queen of Scots – The Fair Devil of Scotland* (London: Star, 1978)

Protz, Roger, *The Story of Brewing in Burton on Trent* (Stroud: The History Press, 2011)

Rollyson, Carl, *Female Icons* (Lincoln NE: iUniverse, Inc., 2005)
Tannahill, Reay, *Fatal Majesty – The Drama of Mary Queen of Scots* (London: BCA, 1998)
Warnicke, Retha M., *Mary Queen of Scots* (Abingdon: Routledge, 2006)
Williams, E. Carleton, *Bess of Hardwick* (London: Longmans, Green & Co. Ltd, 1959)

Index

Visit our website and discover thousands of other History Press books.

www.thehistorypress.co.uk